The Taste of
Ethnographic Things

University of Pennsylvania Press

Contemporary Ethnography Series

Dan Rose and Paul Stoller, General Editors

John D. Dorst. *The Written Suburb: An American Site, An Ethnographic Dilemma.* 1989.

Kirin Narayan. *Storytellers, Saints, and Scoundrels: Folk Narrative in Hindu Religious Teaching.* 1989.

Dan Rose. *Patterns of American Culture: Ethnography and Estrangement.* 1989.

Paul Stoller. *The Taste of Ethnographic Things: The Senses in Anthropology.* 1989.

THE TASTE OF ETHNOGRAPHIC THINGS

The Senses in Anthropology

Paul Stoller

upp

UNIVERSITY OF PENNSYLVANIA PRESS

Philadelphia

Jacket illustration: "Spice Bazaar." Photo by Cheryl Olkes
Frontispiece: "A Lamb Roast in Mehanna, Niger." Photo by the author

Figures 2, 9, photos by Cheryl Olkes. All other figures photos by the author

Portions of Chapter 8 from *Discourse and the Social Life of Meaning,* ed.
P. Chock and J. Wyman. Copyright © 1986 by the Smithsonian Institution.
Reprinted by permission.

Library of Congress Cataloging-in-Publication Data

Stoller, Paul.
  The taste of ethnographic things : the senses in anthropology /
Paul Stoller.
     p.   cm.—(University of Pennsylvania Press contemporary
ethnography series)
  Bibliography: p.
  Includes index.
  ISBN 0-8122-8186-1.—ISBN 0-8122-1292-4 (pbk.)
  1. Songhai (African people) 2. Sense and sensation—Cross-
cultural studies. 3. Ethnology—Niger—Field work. I. Title.
II. Series.
DT547.45.S65S765 1989
306'.096626—dc20   89-33670
Second paperback printing 1990   CIP

For Cheryl

Contents

Illustrations

Acknowledgments

This book is the result of the collective efforts of many people and many institutions. I could not have traveled to Niger over the years without generous support from foundations and U.S. Government Agencies. Fieldwork in 1976–77 was financed through grants from the Fulbright-Hays Doctoral Dissertation Program (G00–76–03659) and from the Wenner-Gren Foundation for Anthropological Research (No. 3175). Research in Niger in 1979–80 was made possible through a NATO Postdoctoral Fellowship in Science. My work in Niger in 1981 and 1982–83 was made possible through grants from the American Philosophical Society and West Chester University. Grants from the Wenner Gren Foundation for Anthropological Research and West Chester University made possible field studies in the summer of 1984. Further grants from West Chester University enabled me to conduct research in Niger in 1985–86 and 1987.

The perspective of this book has been influenced greatly by my graduate studies in sociolinguistics at Georgetown University and in linguistic anthropology at the University of Texas at Austin. At Georgetown Roger Shuy taught me a great deal about the relation between language and society, and Joan Rubin introduced me to anthropology. At the University of Texas at Austin the intellectual guidance offered me by Annette B. Weiner and Joel Sherzer has been invaluable. At the Musée de l'Homme in Paris, Jean Rouch patiently pointed a near-sighted student in the right direction. In Niger, I must honor the memory of the late Seyni Kountché, President of the Republic, who granted me numerous authorizations to conduct ethnographic field research in his country. At the Institut de Recherches en Sciences Humaines I have received warm encouragement and support from Djouldé Laya, Djibo Hamani, and Hamidou Arouna Sidikou, past directors, and Boubé Gado, the present director. After months in the Nigerien bush, Jean-François Berger, Tom and Barbara Hale, Jim and Heidi Lowenthal, Tom Price, the Djibo family, and Kathleen Heffron invited me into their homes and received me with graciousness and kindness.

Many people have commented on the various chapters in this book. In particular I acknowledge the insightful commentary of Jeanne Favret-Saada, Jean-Marie Gibbal, Martin Murphy, Dan Rose, Judith Gleason, John Chernoff, Smadar Lavie, Philip Kilbride, and Norman Whitten, Jr. Members of the staff of the University of Pennsylvania Press, particularly Patricia Smith, have worked with great dedication to transform this project into a fine book. I thank them for their considerable efforts.

I would also like to acknowledge three other people whose work and efforts on my behalf have contributed greatly to the birth of this book. The first is James Fernandez, who has been a continuous source of intellectual support, guidance, and encouragement. The second is Paul Riesman, who died suddenly in 1988. Paul's field site among the Fulani of Burkina Faso was a few hundred kilometers west of mine in Niger. Early on, Paul Riesman saw something in my work that others failed to see. He encouraged me during frustrating times with his unforgettable warmth and kindness. His was an important voice in the anthropological community, and I hope this volume is in a small way a testament to his sense of anthropology. Cheryl Olkes has been involved in my work from its beginning. We have shared many joys in the field and the office. It is through her considerable efforts that this book is readable and coherent.

Lastly, I would like to acknowledge the wisdom of my Songhay teacher, Sohanci Adamu Jenitongo, who died in 1988 at the age of 106. I was privileged to have known him and learned from him. He taught me not only a great deal about Songhay, but a great deal about anthropology as well.

*   *   *

Much of this book consists of previously published material that has been expanded, revised, and updated. An earlier version of Chapter 1 was published as "Bad Sauce, Good Ethnography" in *Cultural Anthropology* 1: 336–52. Chapter 2, "Eye, Mind, and Word in Anthropology," was revised from an article published in the French journal *L'Homme* 24: 93–114. "'Gazing' at the Space of Songhay Politics" was fashioned from two previously published articles, "The Negotiation of Songhay Space: Phenomenology in the Heart of Darkness," *American Ethnologist* 7: 419–31, and "Relativity and the Anthropologist's Gaze," *Anthropology and Humanism Quarterly* 7(4): 2–10. Chapter 4 is a revised version of an article that originally appeared in the *American Ethnologist* 9: 750–62. Material in Chapter 5 was revised from an article that appeared in *Anthropology Quarterly* 60: 114–24. Chapters 6 and 7 were fashioned—with the inclusion of much new information—from one article, "Sound in Songhay Cultural Experience," published in *American Ethnologist* 11: 559–70. Chapter 8 is also a revision of a previously published article. "The Reconstruction of Ethnography" was first delivered as a lecture to the Anthropological Society of Washington in 1983 and then appeared in P. Chock and J. Wyman's edited volume, *Discourse and the Social Life of Meaning* (pp. 51–75), published for the Anthropological Society of Washington by the Smithsonian Institution Press. The material in Chapter 9 has not been previously published.

Today you are learning about us, but to understand us you will have to grow old with us.

Adamu Jenitongo, zima of Tillaberi, Niger

I really do think with my pen, because my head often knows nothing about what my hand is writing.

Wittgenstein

Introduction: A Return to the Senses

In the summer of 1969 I went to the Republic of Niger for the first time. As a recently recruited English teacher, I spent my first two weeks there as a guest of the government. They housed me in a spacious villa and provided me a government chef who had been trained in Paris. My plush air-conditioned quarters protected me from the heat, mosquitoes, and dust of summer in Niger.

This luxurious arrangement initially diverted me from the sensual realities of urban Niger: naked children defecating into the ditches which carried the city's sewage; clouds of aromatic smoke rising from grills on which butchers roasted mouth-watering slices of mutton; dirt roads rendered impassible by rat-infested hills of rotting garbage; gentle winds carrying the pungent smell of freshly pounded ginger; skeletal lepers thrusting their stump-hands in people's faces—their way of asking for money; portly men wrapped in elaborately embroidered blue damask robes, emerging from their Mercedes sedans; blind and crippled beggars, dressed in grimy rags, singing for their meals.

After a two-week dream holiday, I walked into that world and remained there for two years. What did I experience? At first I dove into the sensual world of the city. I was particularly struck by the misery of the "have-nots" juxtaposed with the insouciance of the "haves." The misery of the "have-nots" was at once horrifying and fascinating. It was horrifying because nothing in my twenty-two years of life had prepared me for such human deprivation. It was fascinating for the same reason that makes motorists slow down or stop at the scene of a gruesome automobile accident. The insouciance of the "haves" was also horrifying and fascinating.

How could people with so much be blind to those with so little? At first Africa assailed my senses. I smelled and tasted ethnographic things and was both repelled by and attracted to a new spectrum of odors, flavors, sights, and sounds.

My sensual openness, however, was shortlived. I quickly lost touch with those scenes of abject deprivation which blended into those of insensitive consumption. I soon lost scent of the nose-crinkling stench of the open sewer that gave way to the aromatic aromas of roasting meat. My ears soon deafened to the moans of a sick child that were overwhelmed by the happy laughter of a healthy one. I had become an experience-hardened Africa hand. My immersion in Niger, in Africa, had been, in short, distanciated, intellectualized—taken out of the realm of sensual sentiment. The world of ethnographic things had lost its tastes.

My intellectualist vision compelled me to write about my early experience in Niger for a variety of publications in the United States. It also propelled me toward graduate study, first in linguistics and then in social anthropology. I wanted to master Niger—Africa—by understanding her deeply. My graduate studies sharpened my intellectualist vision and narrowed my sensual horizons. One does fieldwork, I learned, to gather "data" from informants. One collects these data, brings them "home" and then, from an objective distance, analyzes them. The analysis focuses on an intellectual problem—kinship, sociocultural change, symbolic meaning—the solution to which refines social theory. The underlying premise of this epistemology is fundamental: one *can* separate thought from feeling and action.

So I believed when I returned to Niger in 1976 to conduct my doctoral research. My project was to assess the impact of ritual language on local politics among the Songhay. My methods consisted of an assortment of research interventions: a language attitude survey, a census, and tape-recorded linguistic data of everyday interactions and religious ceremonies. My findings would then be used to make a contribution to theory in linguistic anthropology.

In the field, as most anthropologists know,

> The best laid schemes o' mice and men
> Gang aft a-gley.[1]

There is nothing wrong with the conventional research methods I used, but they failed, nonetheless, because most Songhay refused to cooperate with me. They scarcely knew this man who had the temerity to ask strange questions and write down the responses. In fact, my gaze was so narrowly focused in 1976–77 that I missed much of what "went on" during my first year in the field. I had made a number of friends during that period, friends who were impressed by my command of the Songhay language, but despite my linguistic facility they revealed little of themselves to me. When it came time for me to leave, I promised to return, but I don't think many of my friends believed me. For them, one must demonstrate friendship over a long period of time. Then, and only then, do the seeds of trust germinate.

I returned to Niger in 1979–80, 1981, 1982–83, 1984, 1985–86, 1987, and 1988. On each successive trip budding relationships grew into fully rooted friendships, friendships that bore the fruit of trust. Some people admitted to having told me only parts of their stories. Other people asked me to join their families as a "fictive son." Adamu Jenitongo, who became my Songhay "father" and my principal teacher, built me a small mudbrick house in his compound. A few people came to trust me deeply because, in the words of Amadu Zima, an old possession priest, they "liked me, liked me a lot." When I traveled to Niger in March of 1988 to attend Adamu Jenitongo's funeral, the members of his family were deeply moved.

"You came all this way to see Baba?" one of his wives asked.

"Love," I answered, "is something" (*Bakasine hyfo no*).

In fact, it is the play of personalities, the presentation of self, and the presence of sentiment—not only the soundness of conventional research methods—that have become the reasons for my deep immersion into the Songhay world. Slowly, I uncovered an important rule: one cannot separate thought from feeling and action; they are inextricably linked.

This realization opened my senses once again to the world of ethnographic things, to Niger. In 1969 my senses were tuned to the otherness, to the squalor of Niger; my senses of taste, smell, hearing, and sight entered into Nigerien settings. Now I let the sights, sounds, smells, and tastes of Niger flow into me.[2] This fundamental rule in epistemological humility taught me that taste, smell, and hearing are often more important for the Songhay than sight, the privileged sense of the West. In Songhay one can taste kinship, smell witches, and hear the ancestors.

THE STUDY AND RESTUDY OF SONGHAY

The Songhay are a people proud of their past, tracing their origins to the eighth century and the coming of the legendary Aliaman Za to the Niger River basin near the present-day city of Gao, in Mali. Along the banks of the Niger, Za founded the first Songhay dynasty, the Zas; it remained intact until the fourteenth century, when Ali Kolon, who had freed Songhay from the yoke of the Mali Empire, declared a second dynasty, the Sonnis. The Sonni dynasty reached the zenith of its power with the reign of Sonni Ali Ber (1463–91). Sonni Ali Ber expanded the influence and power of Songhay during his epoch. His successor, Askia Mohammed Touré (1493–1528), who founded the third and final Songhay dynasty, the Askiad, bureaucratized the Empire and extended its borders. After the reign of Askia Mohammed the influence and power of the Empire waned. In 1591, the armies of the Moroccan, El Mansur, defeated Songhay and ended the independent rule of what had been a great Sahelian empire.

In the wake of this calamitous defeat, Songhay nobles fled to the south and established a southern empire, which, because of internecine conflicts, was soon balkanized into five principalities. These polities maintained their autonomy until the coming of French armies during the last decade of the nineteenth century.

The Songhay still live along the Niger River basin in western Niger, eastern Mali, and northern Benin. As in the past, they farm millet in most regions and cultivate rice in riverine areas. The society is divided into three general groups of unequal status: the nobles, who trace their descent patrilineally to Askia Mohammed Touré; former slaves, who trace their descent patrilineally to prisoners of precolonial wars; and foreigners, peoples who have migrated into Songhay country in the distant or recent past.

This summary of the historic past and the social present is the result of my study of Songhay society. It is based on both library and field research in 1976–77. My restudies, conducted in 1979–80, 1981, 1982–83, 1984, 1985–86, and 1987 have revealed a great deal more. The tripartite pattern of Songhay social organization has recently been undermined, not by the excesses of colonialism and independence, but by incessant drought, famine, and urban migration. Haunted by dry skies, dusty soil, and barren fields, many Songhay have left the countryside, abandoning in the dust some of their cultural traditions. In the face of this sociocultural dessication, the Songhay nonetheless remember their proud past and maintain their distinct cultural identity.

Besides giving me the perspective to assess social change, long term study of Songhay has plunged me into the Songhay worlds of sorcery and possession, worlds the wisdom of which is closed to outsiders—even Songhay outsiders. My insistence on long term study forced me to confront the interpretative errors of earlier visits. Restudying Songhay also enabled me to get a bit closer to "getting it right." But I have just begun to walk my path. As Adamu Jenitongo once told me, "Today you are learning about us, but to understand us, you will have to grow old with us."

Although restudy has long been a research methodology among French ethnologists, many Anglo-American anthropologists have been content to visit the field one, two, or perhaps three times during their academic careers. This tendency is methodologically disastrous. Like the essays in George Foster's volume *Long Term Field Research in Social Anthropology*, the chapters of this book reflect the methodological and intellectual rewards of long term study in anthropology. This book suggests that one can discover a great many "ethnographic facts" in one year of fieldwork, but it takes years, no matter the perspicacity of the observer, to develop a deep comprehension of others.

Ongoing study of Songhay has also compelled me to tune my senses to the frequencies of Songhay sensibilities. Had I limited my fieldwork in Songhay to one year or two, I would have produced intellectualist tracts, just like the summary above of Songhay history and social organization, in which individual Songhay are "edited out" of the discourse, and in which the sense of sight is prior to those of smell, taste, and sound. Returning to Niger year after year taught me that Songhay use senses other than sight to categorize their sociocultural experience. If anthropologists are to produce knowledge, how can they ignore how their own sensual biases affect the information they produce? This book demonstrates why anthropologists should open their senses to the worlds of their others.

THE SENSES AND ETHNOGRAPHIC WRITING

My rediscovery of the sensual aspects of Songhay social life is unfortunately the exception rather than the rule in the Western academy. For us, dry first principles are generally more important than mouth-watering aromas. It was not always this way, however. In sixteenth-century France savants only rarely used visual metaphors to explain natural phenomena. In fact a number of scholars believe that prior to the eighteenth century the sense of sight was far less developed, cognitively speaking, than those of touch, smell, or hearing.

A case in point brought forward by David Howes concerns the medieval adjudication of claims that a person died a saint.

> Exhuming his body about a year after burial, people discovered in every case that a sweet fragrance rose from the saint's tomb. The flesh had largely vanished from the bones; and the redolence that remained indicated the absence of putrefaction. The pleasing aroma, called the *odor of sanctity, proved* that the saint had miraculously exuviated his flesh. Possessed therefore of an excarnate form rendering him impervious both to desires and to the sins of the flesh, the saint received divine power.[3]

As Howes argues, here is an analysis based on an olfactory as opposed to a visual bias.[4]

This sensualism stood in stark contrast to the ethos of the Middle Ages, throughout which sensualists were considered blasphemers. With the Enlightenment, Suzanne Langer wrote, "the senses, long despised and attributed to the interesting but improper domain of the devil, were recognized as man's most valuable servants, and were rescued from their classical disgrace to wait on him in his new venture."[5] Sense data, especially visual, became all-important to the emerging scientific culture. Empiricism eclipsed rationalism. The emphasis on empirical observation raised sight to a privileged position, soon replacing the bias of the "lower senses" (especially smell and touch).

In medicine, as Foucault reminds us, the coronation of sight occurred in the late eighteenth century. Prior to the emergence of clinical medicine, physicians believed that odor could indicate as well as spread disease. With the advent of anatomy, the body was for the first time "opened up" to the observing eyes of physicians who began to spatialize and categorize tissues, bones, and organs.[6]

In philosophy, Kant's seminal *Critique of Judgment*, published in 1790, was the pioneering effort in the distanciation of observer from observed. In his *Critique* Kant intellectualized and imagined priorities among the senses, relegating smell, taste, and touch to the level of brute as opposed to aesthetic sensation. Combined with the visual intellectualism of the Enlightenment thinkers, the influence of Kant removed Western observers from the arena of sensuality, consequently expunging the so-called lower senses from our discourse, resulting in what Suzanne Langer might have called "reason's disgrace."

Anthropological writers have become full partners in "reason's disgrace." In 1922 Malinowski established the goal of ethnographic writing: to write a document that gives the reader a *sense* of what it is like to live in the lands of others. Although Malinowski's writing was full of dense ethnographic detail, it also featured many sensual passages that described the sights and sounds of Trobriand social life on land and sea.

> Occasionally a wave leaps up and above the platform, and the canoe—unwieldy, square craft as it seems at first—heaves lengthways and crossways, mounting the furrows with graceful agility. When the sail is hoisted, its heavy, stiff folds of golden matting unroll with a characteristic swishing and crackling noise, and the canoe begins to make way; when the water rushes away below with a hiss, and the yellow sail glows against the intense blue of sea and sky—then indeed the romance of sailing seems to open through a new vista.[7]

Since Malinowski's time, however, anthropology has become more and more scientistic. Vivid descriptions of the sensoria of ethnographic situations have been largely overshadowed by a dry, analytical prose. In problem-oriented ethnography, data—excluding in large measure the nonvisual senses—are used to refine aspects of social theory. Lost on this dry steppe of intellectualized prose are characterizations of others as they lead their social lives. Such a trend has unfortunately narrowed the readership for most ethnographies, and has made anthropology a discipline in which practitioners increasingly speak only to each other—not to multiple audiences. One path out of this morass, as I argue in this book, is to write ethnographies that describe the sensual aspects of the field. Such a tack will make us more critically aware of our sensual biases and force us to write ethnographies that combine the strengths of science with the rewards of the humanities.

But "sensual" means more than describing the way things look or smell in the land of the others. The lingering influence of Kant has reinforced our visual orientation to the world. Such visualism, as I have mentioned, can be a Eurocentric mistake for cross-cultural studies of societies in which the senses of taste or smell are more important than vision. Accordingly, several chapters in this book discuss taste, smell, and sound. I suggest that considering the senses of taste, smell, and hearing as much as privileged sight will not only make ethnography more vivid and more accessible, but will render our accounts of others more faithful to the realities of the field—accounts which will then be *more*, rather than less, scientific.

It is also important, however, to redefine our orientation to sight, for anthropologists must learn to assess critically their own gazes. The chapters in Part II, "Visions in the Field," speak to the importance of critical reflection in the field and in the office. A critical doubt reveals to us our perceptual delusions, the source of many of the profound misinterpretations that undermine so many anthropological representations of others.[8]

The works of James Clifford and George Marcus, among others, have cast a critical doubt on anthropological and ethnographic praxis. This body of work has forced anthropologists to consider the representation of others as a major disciplinary problem.[9] This writing, however, often suffers from discombobulation. Critical writers consider the rarefied problems of philosophy and aesthetics in the human sciences with limited reference to real people in real situations—in our case, the play of problems in the field.[10] The chapters in this book illustrate the benefits of grounding our theoretical ruminations in descriptive ethnography. In this way theory—science—is *not* repudiated, but is reduced to a non-reified tool which helps to unravel the tangled cultural mysteries of other societies.

A FOUR COURSE MEAL

This book is divided into four parts. Part I, "Tastes," consists of one chapter, "The Taste of Ethnographic Things," an essay on taste and smell, elements of sensual experience which are generally ignored in ethnographic discourse. Here I demonstrate not only how taste and smell are central ingredients in the recipe of Songhay social relations, but also why most Western writers would consider these ethnographic spices tasteless additions to the sauce of Songhay ethnography.

Part II, "Visions in the Field," the longest section of the book, consists of four chapters on my perception of the Songhay and their perception of me. In Chapter 2, "Eye, Mind, and Word in Anthropology," I discuss how and why Western "intellectualism" has impoverished our visual perception. I call on anthropologists to adopt "the painter's gaze." " 'Gazing' at the Space of Songhay Politics," Chapter 3, considers how the privileged sense of vision influenced my perception of things Songhay, prompting me on numerous occasions to see social patterns that did not exist. My ability to "read" Songhay interaction is considered in Chapter 4, "Signs in the Social Order: Riding a Songhay Bush Taxi." If ethnographers want to be able to "see" the deep significance of everyday interaction, I argue, they must return to the field year after year. In Chapter 5, "Son of Rouch: Songhay Visions of the Other," the ethnographic world of vision is turned upside down. Here, Songhay images of the ethnographer-as-European are highlighted.

Part III, "Sounds in Cultural Experience," consists of two chapters. The role of sound as a vital force in Songhay possession ceremonies is probed in Chapter 6, "Sound in Songhay Possession." Here the consequences of taking an auditory as opposed to a visual orientation to the world are considered in the ethnographic context of Songhay possession. In Chapter 7 the same auditory orientation is used to examine the physical power of words in Songhay sorcery.

There are but two chapters in Part IV, "The Senses in Anthropology." In Chapter 8, "The Reconstruction of Ethnography," I consider the philosophical underpinnings of the anthropological "episteme" and demonstrate how the decaying principles of the Western metaphysic have shaped what we see, how we think, what we say and how we write. Chapter 9, "Detours," advocates the phenomenological return to things themselves—to poetry, to conversations with others as well as ourselves.

*   *   *

Taken together, the chapters in this book speak to two important and integrated issues germane to the future course of anthropological research and representation. The first is methodological. The book demonstrates the considerable scientific rewards of the long term study of one society. Breakthroughs in the apprehension of Songhay space and realizations of the importance of sound and taste in Songhay cultural categorization occurred only after repeated visits to Niger over a period of years. Breakthroughs occurred because I mastered the language during those years and established lasting friendships built on a foundation of mutual trust.

Long term study of the Songhay also revealed to me epistemological biases which produced serious errors of interpretation and representation. Recognition of these errors led me to the second issue illustrated in this book: the sensualization of my approach to the study and representation of Songhay. This book represents the intellectual context for my ethnographic work (*In Sorcery's Shadow* [1987] and *Fusion of the Worlds* [1989]), in which I try to represent faithfully the complexities—sensual and otherwise—of Songhay society and culture. As a complex, this work strives to realize the simple but ever-difficult goal that Malinowski long ago set for our discipline: to produce an ethnographic literature that gives readers a taste of ethnographic things.

PART I

Tastes in Anthropology

Some books are to be tasted, others to be swallowed, some few to be chewed and digested.

F. Bacon

1 | *The Taste of Ethnographic Things*

All meats that can endure it I like rare, and I like them high, even to the point of smelling bad in many cases.[1]

Montaigne

Like other peoples in Sahelian West Africa, the Songhay take great pride in their hospitality. "A guest is God in your house," goes the Songhay adage, and so when strangers are accepted as guests in most Songhay compounds they receive the best of what their hosts can afford to offer. The host displaces his own kin from one of his houses and gives it to the guest. He removes the mattress from his bed and gives it to the guest. And then he orders the kinswoman who prepares the family meals to make her best sauces for the guest.

In 1984 Paul Stoller, an anthropologist, and Cheryl Olkes, a sociologist, traveled to Niger to conduct a study of the medicinal properties of plants used in Songhay ethnomedicine. Since both Stoller and Olkes were seasoned fieldworkers among the Songhay, they had experienced the pleasures of Songhay hospitality. And so when they came to the compound of Adamu Jenitongo, in Tillaberi, they were not surprised when Moussa, one of Adamu Jenitongo's sons, insisted that they stay in his mudbrick house. They were not surprised when Adamu Jenitongo, an old healer whom Stoller had known for fifteen years, gave them his best straw mattresses. "You will sleep well on these," he told them. They were not surprised when the old healer told Djebo, the wife of his younger son, Moru, to prepare fine sauces for them.

Stoller and Olkes had come to Tillaberi to discuss the medicinal prop-

Figure 1: Preparation of "kilshi" at the market in Mehanna, Niger

erties of plants with Adamu Jenitongo, perhaps the most knowledgeable healer in all of western Niger. They planned to stay in Tillaberi for two weeks and them move on to Mehanna and Wanzerbé, two villages in which Stoller had won the confidence of healers. During the two weeks in Tillaberi, Stoller and Olkes ate a variety of foods and sauces. Some days they ate rice with black sauce (*hoy bi*) for lunch and rice with a tomato-based sauce flavored with red pepper and sorrel for dinner. Some days they ate rice cooked in a tomato sauce (*suruundu*) for lunch and millet paste with peanut sauce for dinner. All of these sauces contained meat, a rare ingredient in most Songhay meals. When Songhay entertain Europeans—Stoller and Olkes, for example—the staples of the diet do not change, but the quality of the sauces does. Europeans are guests in Songhay compounds; people do not prepare tasteless sauces for them!

People in the neighborhood had the same perception: "They have come

to visit Adamu Jenitongo again. There will be good food in the compound."
In good times a host spares no expense. In bad times Stoller and Olkes
quietly slipped Adamu Jenitongo money so he could fulfill his ideal behavior.

The arrival of Stoller and Olkes in Tillaberi that year, in fact, was a
bright beacon that attracted swarms of the "uninvited" in search of savory
sauces. At lunch and dinner time visitors would arrive and linger, knowing
full well that the head of a Songhay household is obliged to feed people who
happen to show up at meal times.

The "men who came to dinner" were so many that poor Djebo had to
double the amount of food she normally prepared. Djebo was a mediocre
cook, but the uninvited guests didn't seem to mind as they stuffed their
mouths with rice, meat, and sauce.

There was one particular guest, whom everyone called *Gao Boro* (literally "the man from Gao"), who unabashedly came to breakfast, lunch, and
dinner every day of Stoller and Olkes' visit. This man, a refugee (or was it a
fugitive?) from Gao, in the Republic of Mali, had been living hand-to-
mouth in Tillaberi for four months. He had perfected a terrific rent scam to
cut his expenses. In Tillaberi, landlords will let their properties to anyone
who promises to pay the rent money at the end of the month. Paying at the
end of the first month is a matter of Songhay honor. At the time of our visit,
Gao Boro was on his third house. When a landlord would come for his
money, *Gao Boro* would say he was broke. The owner would throw him out,
and *Gao Boro* would find another unsuspecting landlord. Stoller and Olkes
soon realized the direct relationship between *Gao Boro*'s neighborliness—
he lived 50 meters from Adamu Jenitongo's compound—and his ability to
stretch his food budget.

Most people in the compound were reasonably happy with the food in
1984. Adamu Jenitongo's wives—Jemma and Hadjo—did complain about
the toughness of the meat. So did Adamu Jenitongo. The problem, of
course, was that Djebo refused to tenderize the meat—which had come
from local stock—before cooking it in the sauce. Olkes suggested that
Djebo marinate the meat. Djebo smiled at Olkes and ignored her advice.
The toughness of the meat notwithstanding, everyone ate Djebo's sauces—
until the last day of Stoller and Olkes' visit, when Djebo served bad sauce.

The last day in Tillaberi had been exhausting. Stoller had had two long
sessions with Adamu Jenitongo during which they discussed the medicinal
properties of plants and the Songhay philosophy of healing. Olkes had seen
people in town and at the market. She had walked a good eight kilometers
under the relentless Sahelian sun. At dusk, they each washed in the bath
house: a three-foot-high square mudbrick enclosure equipped with a stool,

Figure 2: Spice bazaar (photo by Cheryl Olkes)

a five-liter bucket, soap, and a plastic mug. Refreshed, they sat on one of their straw mattresses and waited for Djebo. Smiling, she brought them a large casserole of rice and a small one of sauce, set them at their feet, and gave them two spoons. When Stoller opened the small casserole, a sour odor overwhelmed them. Stoller saw the nightly procession of uninvited guests sauntering into the compound. Olkes wrinkled her nose.

"What is it?"

"It's *fukko hoy* [a sauce made by boiling the leaves of the fukko plant]," Stoller said.

"*Fukko hoy?*"

Stoller stirred the sauce with his spoon; it was meatless. "Shine your flashlight on the sauce, will you?" Stoller asked Olkes.

Olkes' flashlight revealed a viscous green liquid. "You can take the first taste," Olkes told Stoller.

"Wait a minute." Stoller picked up the small casserole and poured some of the *fukko hoy* over the rice. He put a spoonful of the rice and sauce into his mouth. "It's the worst damn sauce I've ever eaten," he told Olkes. "Straight *fukko hoy* seasoned with salt and nothing else!"

Olkes tasted the rice and sauce. "It's absolutely awful."

Like diplomats, Olkes and Stoller ate a little bit of the meal before pushing the casseroles away. Other people in the compound were less polite. Saying the sauce smelled and tasted like bird droppings, Moru, Djebo's husband, took his rice and sauce and dumped it in the compound garbage pit, a two-foot-deep hole about six feet in diameter that was littered with date palm pits, orange rinds, gristle, bones, and trash. "Let the goats eat this crap," he said.

Jemma, one of Adamu Jenitongo's two wives, said: "This sauce shames us. Djebo has brought great shame upon this compound." Hadjo, Adamu Jenitongo's other wife, echoed Jemma's comments. "How could anyone prepare so horrible a sauce for the guests in our compound?"

Gao Boro, the refugee-fugitive from Mali, arrived for his nightly "European" meal. He took one taste of the bad sauce, stood up and declared: "I refuse to eat sauce that is not fit for an animal. I'm going to Halidou's for *my* dinner tonight." From everyone's perspective, the bad sauce was in bad taste.

THE ETIOLOGY OF BAD SAUCE

Djebo, a young Fulan (Peul) woman, came to live in Adamu Jenitongo's compound in the summer of 1982.[2] She had formed an attachment to Moru, a drummer in the possession cult, and had spent months following him to possession ceremonies. Eventually, she moved in with him—shameless behavior for a never-married 15-year-old girl. Still considered too young for marriage (most Songhay men do not marry until they are 30) 21-year-old Moru was a musician whose earnings were erratic. When he did have money it flew from his hands, which were always open to his "friends." Moru and Djebo brought much shame to Adamu Jenitongo's compound. Although first-time brides are not expected to be virgins, they are expected to avoid shaming their families. Adamu Jenitongo could have asked Djebo to leave, but he did not. By the time Stoller arrived in December 1982, Djebo was visibly pregnant. Now, all the neighbors could see that Djebo and Moru had been living in sin. What to do? One option was abortion, a longstanding though unpopular Songhay practice. Another option was to send Djebo home to have her "fatherless" child, the usual Songhay practice. The final option was, of course, marriage. No one wanted an abortion. Moru wanted to marry his love. Adamu Jenitongo and his wives wanted the pregnant girl to return to her mother's compound.

During Stoller's visit, there were many arguments in the compound about Moru and Djebo.

"What would you do with her?" Adamu Jenitongo asked Stoller.

"You're asking me?"

"Moru should marry a Songhay woman," Adamu Jenitongo stated. "He should marry one of the girls from our home near Simiri. If he marries one of our people, everyone will be happy. Do you not agree?" he asked Stoller.

Concealing his uneasiness, Stoller said that he agreed.

Moru, who had been inside his hut, overheard the discussion between Stoller and his father and ran out to confront them.

"And what about me, Baba? Doesn't anyone ask me, Moru, about my feelings? I want Djebo. I want to marry her. I want her to have my child."

Adamu Jenitongo scoffed at Moru. "Marry her! First you bring this Fulan woman into my compound. Then you make her pregnant, and now you want to marry the worthless bitch." Adamu Jenitongo turned to Stoller. "What is this world coming to? The young people have no respect." He turned now to Moru. "You live in my household, you eat my food, you learn from me our heritage, but you have no heart and no mind. You are still a child."

Moru stormed off to his hut, fuming. Jemma, his mother, returned from the market with meat and spices. Hadjo, her co-wife, informed her of the most recent confrontation in the compound. Jemma looked at Stoller.

"Don't you think it is wrong for that worthless Fulan woman to be here? Look at her," she said loudly, pointing at the girl, who was sitting on the threshold of Moru's hut. "She's pregnant, but she's here with us. Pregnant women must live with their mothers so they give birth to healthy babies. Does that worthless Fulan do this? No! She sits here. She follows Moru to possession dances. Sometimes she walks for hours—she and the baby in her belly."

"Is this bad?" Stoller asked Jemma.

"They say that a mother who wanders with a baby in her belly will produce a monster child. That worthless Fulan is breeding a monster. I am certain of it."

"She should be with her mother," Hadjo reiterated.

During Stoller's visit there were also daily arguments between Jemma, Moru's mother, and Ramatu, Djebo's mother. On one occasion Ramatu attempted to drag her daughter back to her compound. Djebo broke her mother's grip and cursed her. Jemma cursed Djebo for cursing her mother. And Ramatu cursed Jemma for cursing her daughter. As the two older women traded ethnic slurs in Songhay, Fulan, and Hausa, a sobbing Djebo told Moru, her love, that she was walking into the bush to die. Since no one took Djebo at her word, they watched her walk toward the mountain. Ramatu returned to her compound, Jemma got back to her food preparations, and Moru went into his hut.

Two hours passed and Djebo had not returned. Moru entered Stoller's hut. "Should we go and look for her?"

"I think so, Moru."

Stoller and Moru left to search for Djebo. They returned with her two hours later. Everyone in the compound scolded the young girl.

"You are a hardheaded bitch," Jemma said.

"You are a worthless Fulan, who brings us heartache," Adamu Jenitongo said.

Djebo cried and Moru followed her into his hut.

When Stoller and Olkes returned to Adamu Jenitongo's compound in 1984, a child no more than a year and a half old waddled over to them. Laterite dust powdered her body. Mucus had caked on her upper lip.

"That's my daughter, Jamilla," Moru proclaimed.

Jamilla burst into tears when Olkes approached her.

"She's not used to white people," Jemma said.

"She's a monster child," Hadjo declared.

The term "monster child" swept Stoller back to his previous visit and the long discussions that had raged about women who wander when they are pregnant. Had the prediction come true?

"And no wonder," said Jemma, "with a mother who wandered the countryside with a child in her belly."

Moru told Stoller that he and Djebo were married shortly after his departure the previous year.

"And you didn't write?" Stoller joked.

Moru shrugged. Djebo pounded millet next to the compound's second mudbrick house, which Moru had built for his family. "Djebo," Moru called to his wife, "prepare a fine meal for them. They are tired from their trip, and we must honor them."

Adamu Jenitongo gave Djebo money and told her to go to the market and buy good spices and a good cut of meat. Djebo took the money and frowned. When she had left, Moussa (Adamu Jenitongo's other son), Jemma, and Moru complained about her. She was lazy. She was quarrelsome. They didn't trust her. She didn't know how to cook—probably because she hadn't listened to her mother long enough to learn. When she prepared meat it was so tough that even Moru couldn't chew it. The sauces were tasteless even though Adamu Jenitongo gave her money to buy the best spices. But no one had done anything to improve the domestic situation.

"Why don't you teach her how to cook?" Olkes asked.

"Hah," Jemma snorted. "She doesn't want to learn."

"Why don't you show her the right spices to buy?" Olkes persisted.

"She doesn't care. She doesn't care," Jemma answered.

Olkes felt sorry for Djebo. She was, after all, a teenager living among people who seemed set against her and who bore longstanding prejudice against her ethnic group. As the youngest affine in the compound, moreover, Djebo was expected not only to cook, but to buy food in the market, take care of her infant, fetch water from a neighborhood pump, clean pots and pans, and do the laundry. From dawn to dusk, Djebo performed these tasks as Jemma and Hadjo sat in front of their huts and criticized her.

Olkes decided to befriend Djebo. She accompanied Djebo to the pump and to the market. On market day, Olkes bought Djebo a black shawl, the current rage in Tillaberi. For whatever reason—culture, age, or personality—Djebo did not respond to these overtures. She socialized outside of the compound and did not participate in the rambling conversations of the early evening.

One day before Stoller and Olkes' departure, Djebo prepared a wonderful sauce for the noon meal. She made a locust bean sauce flavored with peanut flour. Olkes and Stoller ate with abandon. When Djebo came to their house to collect the empty casseroles, Olkes complimented her on the meal.

Stoller raised his arms skyward and said: "Praise be to God."

Saying nothing, Djebo smiled and left their house. Thirty minutes later, Djebo returned to see Stoller and Olkes—her first social visit in two weeks. Saying little, she looked over their things. She opened the lid of their non-fat dry milk and tasted some. She touched their camera, and ran her fingers over their tape recorder. Olkes and Stoller had seen this kind of behavior before. A person in Niger rarely asks for money directly; rather, he or she lingers in the donor's house and says nothing. Djebo lingered in Stoller and Olkes' house for thirty minutes and left.

"Do you understand the reason for that scrumptious meal?" Olkes asked Stoller.

Stoller nodded. "She isn't satisfied with the black shawl?"

"I guess not."

"Damn her! We can't give her money. We have to give money to Adamu Jenitongo."

"She doesn't want to follow the rules of custom, does she?"

"I just bet that she has been pocketing some of the money given to her for food," Stoller said. "That's why the sauces have been mediocre."

That night Djebo's horrible *fukko hoy* expressed sensually her anger, an anger formed from a complex of circumstances. She wanted her sauce to be disgusting.

THE ETIOLOGY OF TASTE

Djebo prepared a sauce to be rejected, cast away, spit out. Put another way, Djebo's sauce was the symbolic equivalent of vomit, something that our bodies reject. In the most literal sense Djebo's sauce was distasteful.

How does Djebo's sour sauce—her calculated distastefulness—fit with the conception of Taste in the Western philosophical tradition? In a word, it is different; it is non-theoretical.

One of the earliest writers on taste was Seneca. In his *Epistulae morales* he wrote that food not only nourishes our bodies, but also

> nourishes our higher nature,—we should see to it that whatever we have absorbed should not be allowed to remain unchanged, or it will be no part of us. We must digest it; otherwise it will merely enter memory and not the reasoning power. Let us loyally welcome such foods and make them our own, so that something that is one may be formed out of many elements.[3]

Seneca was among the first of the classical philosophers to write of judgment with digestive metaphors. "For Seneca, the proper digestion of received ideas both educates and is the result of an independent faculty of judgment, and this in turn is the precondition of right action."[4] These metaphors stem from the classical notion that the mouth and tongue enable us to "ingest" the outside world. Physical tasting is extended to mental tasting, the classical notion of judgment.[5]

In his *Critique of Judgment*, Kant rejects the classical notion that the faculty of taste can be extended to social, political, or scientific matters. In fact, he removes taste entirely from the domain of science, preferring to consider it a purely aesthetic sense.

> In order to distinguish whether anything is beautiful or not, we refer the representation, not by the understanding to the object for cognition, but by imagination (perhaps in conjunction with the understanding) to the subject and its feeling of pleasure and pain. The judgment of taste is therefore not a judgment of cognition, and is consequently not logical but aesthetical, by which we understand that those determining grounds can be *no other than subjective.*[6]

Kant's passage suggests that the faculty of taste should be restricted to the apprehension of objects of beauty. Following the publication of the *Critique of Judgment* in 1790, taste was no longer considered an appropriate concept in the classically approved domains of politics, society and science—domains that were restricted to the logical, objective, and scientific reflection of the Enlightenment.

The Etymology of Taste in English
Raymond Williams writes that the word taste came into the English language around the thirteenth century, but that its earliest meaning was closer to "touch" or "feel."[7] "Taste" comes to us from the Old French *taster*, and from the Italian *tastare*, which translates to "feel, handle, or touch."

"Good taast" in the sense of good understanding was recorded in 1425.[8] But the metaphoric extensions of the word became confused in the latter part of the seventeenth century and the eighteenth century, when it was associated with general rules. In English, then, the sensual aspects of taste were gradually replaced by the more general and rule-governed notion. Perhaps due to the Kantian influence, the meanings of *taste* and *good taste* are even today far removed from their sensual attributes. Djebo's sense of taste is sensual and subjective; Kant's sense of Taste is rarefied and objective.

The Sensual Tastes of Montaigne

Djebo's non-theoretical sense of taste is similar to Montaigne's. The final section of his *Essais*, entitled "Of Experience," is a compendium of Montaigne's physical tastes: what he likes to eat, how often he likes to eat, how much he likes to eat. In this final book, Montaigne discusses his sleeping habits, his kidney stones, his medicines, his squeamishness, his hatred of sweets as a child and his love of sweets as an adult, his digestion, his indigestion, and even his bowel movements. On the subject of bowels, Montaigne also writes that "both Kings and philosophers defecate, and ladies too. . . . Wherefore I will say this about that action: that we should relegate it to certain prescribed nocturnal hours, and force and subject ourselves to them by habit, as I have done."[9] Montaigne's "father hated all kinds of sauces; I love them all. Eating too much bothers me; but I have as yet no really certain knowledge that any kind of food intrinsically disagrees with me."[10] Alas, Montaigne never ate Djebo's *fukko hoy*.

Derrida's Dregs

Montaigne's sensuality has had a minimal influence on Western thought, however. More prevalent today are the rarefied Enlightenment metaphors of composition and construction. In Hegel's constructive system, for example, "the material of ideality is light and sound. Voice, in the relation to hearing (the most sublime sense), animates sound, permitting the passage from more sensible existence to the representational existence of the concept."[11] Sight and hearing are theoretical senses that represent the attempt of the Enlightenment philosophers to create from the chaos of appearances constructed systems of "reality," wherein one might Taste the Truth.

In sharp contrast to historical and modern masters of philosophy, Derrida stands for sensuality as opposed to rarefaction, for deconstructionism as opposed to constructionism, for decomposition as opposed to Taste. In *Of Grammatology* and in *Glas*, Derrida indicates a philosophical system based upon such non-theoretical senses as taste (also smell and touch) which depend upon a part of the body, the tongue, which is primary in speech production:

The dividing membrane which is called the soft palate, fixed by its upper edge to the border of the roof, *floats* freely, at its lower end, above the base of the tongue. Its two lateral sides (it is a quadrilateral) are called "pillars." In the middle of the floating end, at the entrance to the throat, hangs the fleshy appendage of the uvula, like a small grape. The text is spit out. It is like a discourse in which the unities model themselves after an excrement, a secretion. And because it has to do here with a glottic gesture, the tongue working on itself, *saliva* is the element which sticks the unities together.[12]

As Ulmer suggests, Derrida's texts condemn Hegel's assertion that odor and taste "are useless for artistic pleasure, given that esthetic contemplation requires objectivity without reference to desire or will, whereas 'things present themselves to smell only to the degree in which they are constituted by a process, in which they dissolve into the air with practical effects.'"[13] For Derrida there should be no separation of the intelligible from the sensible. Since Kant, he argues, Taste has been an objective, rarefied distancing from an object of art. Using the sensual Montaigne as one of his models, Derrida opposes *gustus* with disgust and taste with distaste. The key concept of Derrida's writing on taste is *le vomi*, "which explicitly engages not the 'objective' senses of hearing and sight, nor even touch, which Kant describes as 'mechanical,' all three of which involve perception of or at surfaces, but the 'subjecive' or 'chemical' senses of taste and smell."[14] For Derrida, then, Djebo's *fukko hoy* should not only be spit out into an ethnographic text, but should be done so with sensual vividness, for Djebo's bad sauce is gloriously disgusting; it reeks with meaning.

Taste in Anthropology

Beyond the sensual descriptions in anthropological cookbooks, most anthropologists have followed Hegel's lead in separating the intelligible from the sensible. This Hegelian tendency is evident from even a cursory examination of ethnographic writing. Like most writers, most ethnographers tacitly conform to a set of conventions that colleagues use to judge a work. Marcus and Cushman have suggested that conventions governing ethnographic representation devolve from realism. They argue that realist ethnographic discourse seeks the reality of the whole of a given society, and that "realist ethnographies are written to allude to the whole by means of parts or foci of analytical attention which constantly evoke a social and cultural totality."[15] In an article in *L'Homme*, Stoller describes the philosophical development of realism in ethnography.[16] That development eventually resulted in a set of conventions that Marcus and Cushman have analyzed:

1. a narrative structure which devolves from cultural, functionalist, or structuralist analytical categories to achieve a total ethnography;

2. a third person narrative voice which distinguishes realist ethnographies from travel accounts;

3. a manner of presentation in which individuals among the people studied remain nameless, characterless;

4. a section of text, usually a Preface or Afterword, which describes the context of investigation;

5. a focus on everyday life contexts representing the Other's reality to justify the fit of the analytical framework to the ethnographic situation;

6. an assertion that the ethnography represents the native's point of view;

7. a generalizing style in which events are rarely described idiosyncratically, but as typical manifestations of marriage, kinship, ritual, etc.;

8. a use of jargon which signals that the text is, indeed, an ethnography as opposed to a travel account;

9. a reticence by authors to discuss their competence in the Other's language.[17]

While most ethnographers religiously followed these conventions of realist representation in the past, there are a growing number of scholars who are worried about the epistemological and political ramifications of ethnographic realism. Directly and indirectly, their ethnographic and theoretical writings reflect these philosophic issues.[18] Fabian writes of his concern about anthropology's intellectual imperialism: "Perhaps I failed to make it clear that I wanted language and communication to be understood as a kind of praxis in which the Knower cannot claim ascendency over the Known (nor, for that matter, one Knower over another). As I see it now, the anthropologist and his interlocuters only 'know' when they meet each other in one and the same contemporality."[19]

Although the new "experimental" works have been provocative, most of them consider typical anthropological subjects of study, albeit through partially altered conventions of representation. How could it be otherwise, when disciplinary constraints force most writers to concentrate on certain kinds of subjects: the theory of Taste instead of the taste of bad sauce, the theory of the family instead of texts that familiarize the reader with family members, the theory of experimental ethnography instead of experimental ethnographies. How can it be otherwise, when disciplinary constraints impose form and order on what is published. Take, for example, the *Abstracts of the Annual [Anthropology] Meetings:*

> Name, institution, and title of paper or film must precede narrative portion: Put last name first; use capital letters for author's last name and title of paper; do

not include 'university' or 'college' with institution name given in parenthe-
ses. . . . Write the text in complete sentences. Use the present tense; use only
third person.[20]

In addition, the American Anthropological Association gives prospective
participants some useful tips on writing a "good abstract":

> A "good" abstract should be an informative summary of a longer work. It
> should state the central topic at the beginning; it should clearly indicate the
> nature and extent of the data on which it is based; it should outline the nature of
> the problem or issue and delineate the relevant scientific argument; and it
> should show how the content relates to the existing literature. Where helpful,
> citations may be used. The abstract must be typed *double spaced*, and it must fit
> *within* the box provided below.[21]

This prescription may be a fine model for terse scientific writing, but it
discourages unconventionality in ethnographic writing with the message
it sends to potential Annual Meeting participants: "We are a scientific
organization. We sponsor scientific papers in our scientific program." Good
or "beautiful" abstracts, in the sense of Kant and Hegel, are written in the
present tense (the ethnographic present?) and in the third person (a marker
of objectivity?) Even today, Hegel's *Esthetics* casts a long shadow over
anthropological representation.

Despite the difficulties precipitated by a long entrenched philosophical tradition, it is altogether certain that the pioneering and courageous
efforts of contemporary ethnographers have forced anthropologists to ponder the nature of both their scholarship and their being. But do these
writers take us far enough? Are there other dimensions of ethnographic
discourse, other conventions of representation which may carry anthropology deeper into the being of the others? Are there other modes of representation that better solve the fundamental problems of realist ethnographic
representation: voice, authority, and authenticity?

TASTEFUL ETHNOGRAPHY

How does a piece of ethnographic writing get published? Here the digestive
metaphors are particularly relevant. An author submits her or his manuscript to a publisher or to a journal. Editors ingest the manuscript. If the
material falls within the conventions of representation of a discipline, the
editors are likely to digest what they have taken in and the manuscript will
eventually be published. If the material violates those conventions, the
editors may well find the piece hard to swallow and the manuscript is
returned to the author, a case of Derrida's *vomi*. Indeed, when editors write
comments to authors of rejected (vomited) manuscripts, they often suggest
how the author might transform his or her piece from disgusting vomit into

digestible food for thought. Examples of these comments from Stoller's files illustrate how readers and editors reinforce conventional anthropological tastes.

Example 1 [Letter from acquisitions editor to Stoller]. I have just received two reviews of your manuscript, and I'm sorry to have to tell you that these have not been sufficiently encouraging for me to feel able to offer to consider the work further. Both reviewers thought that the script contained some interesting data, but felt that the theoretical argument was insufficiently well developed.

Example 2 [Comments from Stoller to anonymous author]. The author of this article suggests that anthropologists consider music more seriously, less tangentially, in their analyses of sociocultural systems. Merriman made more or less the same statement in his pioneering *Anthropology of Music* (1964), which the author unfortunately does not cite. . . . The author leads one to believe that we should consider the sociocultural aspects of music seriously. I fully agree. After reading the piece, however, I feel the author has fallen into the trap he/she says other anthropologists have fallen into. Music is not the central concern of this article; it is of secondary or perhaps tertiary importance when compared with the author's overriding concern with subsistence and the materialist perspective. . . . In short the author fails to highlight the importance of music in the cultural scheme of things. . . .

Example 3 [Comments of Stoller to anonymous author]. In this piece the reader is treated to a plethora of excellent ethnography in which the author develops the sociological context of x's name change. But the author does not blend this rich material with other studies in Africa or elsewhere which are on similar topics. . . . What kind of contribution does this piece make to ethnological theory, method, compared to other works on the topic? . . .

Example 4 [Reader's comments to Stoller]. I sympathize with the author's desire to go beyond the limits of positivism and enter into the mental set of the people he studies, though he might take note that this is the point of departure espoused by such diverse scholars as Boas, Malinowski, and Radin, among others. My objection to the work is not in his effort to seek an inside viewpoint, but in his failure to demonstrate its value, and, above all, in his failure to meet the canons of academic evidence. One must presume that the young man in his narrative was himself—but his unwillingness to communicate in the scientific mode and to adhere to the Songhay rules, deprives us of direct evidence for this insight and makes us wonder at the source and character of his information.

Example 5 [Reader's comments to Stoller]. This is basically a suitable article for the . . . , since it has an interesting and significant point to make concerning the need to recognize the importance of sound in many societies. I feel, however, that many readers would not be gripped enough at the beginning of the article [a narrative with dialogue] . . . to see it through to the end. . . . My personal preference is for less humanistic and subjective language.

Example 6 [Reader's comments on Stoller's manuscript]. . . . There is no question that the subject matter is important and underrepresented in the literature, or that the author has some very valuable field data in hand. It would be quite useful to have a good study of Songhay religion and culture. . . . While there is some interesting description of possession rituals, and of Songhay religion and history, if I have to judge it frankly I must say that at this point it is a half-baked manuscript.

The weakness of its theoretical grounding leads to the lack of any real integration of the descriptive material beyond the repeated (and ultimately somewhat boring) assertion that the cults are forms of cultural resistance. . . . I think there are two central points of weakness, which the author glides over at the beginning where he casually dismisses psychological and functional accounts: he shows no evidence of having read the work of Victor Turner . . . and he shows no evidence of familiarity with the *recent* studies of the psychophysiology of trance which have made such rapid advances in our understanding of these phenomena. . . .

And so it goes in the modern era of anthropology, an era that in many ways is past its shelflife.[22] One way of freeing ourselves from the constraints of Taste in Anthropology is to engage fully in a tasteful ethnography. Freed from the social, political, and epistemological constraints of realism, a tasteful ethnography would take us beyond the mind's eye and into the domain of the senses of smell and taste. Such an excursion into sensuality would complement the rarefied Hegelian senses of sight and sound.

Tasteful Fieldwork

In tasteful fieldwork, anthropologists would not only investigate kinship, exchange, and symbolism, but also describe with literary vividness the smells, tastes, and textures of the land, the people, and the food. Rather than looking for deep-seated hidden truths, the tasteful fieldworker understands, following Foucault, "that the deep hidden meaning, the unreachable heights of truth, the murky interiors of consciousness are all shams."[23] From the sensual tasteful vantage, the fieldworker investigates the life stories of individual Songhay, Nuer, or Trobrianders as opposed to totalized investigations of the Songhay, the Nuer, or the Trobriander. This recording of the complexities of the individual's social experience lends texture to the landscape of the fieldworker's notes. In this way, seemingly insignificant incidents as being served bad sauce become as important as sitting with a nameless informant and recording genealogies—data—that eventually become components in a system of kinship. In this way ethnographic research creates voice, authority, and an aura of authenticity.

Tasteful Writing

There are probably many anthropologists who do engage in tasteful fieldwork. Despite their scientific objectives, they become sensually immersed in their field surroundings. These impressions, however, are usually cast aside—becoming vomit—in their published theoretical and ethnographic writings. Like Djebo's bad sauce, conventions of representation governing genre selection could be thrown into a trash pit.

Acknowledging the diverse collection of refuse, the tasteful writer uses the notion of melange as his or her guiding metaphor for producing tasteful ethnographic writing.

In Derrida's *Glas*, the writing on the pages is arranged in two columns. In the left-hand column is prose representing Hegel (rarefaction, Taste, the Enlightenment and its theoretical senses). In the right-hand column, by contrast, is prose representing Genet (sensuality, taste, post-modernism and its non-theoretical senses). Within this revolutionary stylistics is a powerful indirect challenge to the fundamental metaphors of the Western philosophic tradition. Derrida's *Glas* is in bad Taste. But Derrida's bad Taste—his vomit—provides a point of reference for tasteful ethnographic writing that incorporates the non-theoretical senses.

Consider first an example from James Agee's *Let Us Now Praise Famous Men*, in which he describes the odors of a tenant farm house in Alabama.

> These are its ingredients. The odor of pine lumber, wide thin cards of it, heated in the sun, in no way doubled or insulated, in closed and darkened air. The odor of woodsmoke, the fuel being again mainly pine, but in part also, hickory, oak and cedar. The odors of cooking. Among these, most strongly, the odors of fried salt pork and of fried and boiled pork lard, and second, the odor of cooked corn. The odors of sweat in many stages of age and freshness, this sweat being a distillation of pork, lard, corn, woodsmoke, pine and ammonia. The odors of sleep, of bedding and of breathing, for the ventilation is poor. The odors of all the dirt that in the course of time can accumulate in a quilt and mattress. Odors of staleness from clothes hung or stored away, not washed. I should further describe the odor of corn: in sweat, or on the teeth and the breath, when it is eaten as much as they eat it, it is of a particular sweet stuffy fetor, to which the nearest parallel is the odor of the yellow excrement of a baby. . . .[24]

Consider next an example from John Chernoff's *African Rhythm and African Sensibility*, in which he describes how music and African social life interpenetrate.

> At the beginning of each year the *harmattan* winds blow a fine dust from the Sahara Desert across the Sudan and over the coastal areas of the Gulf of Guinea. In Bamako, capital of Mali, you might observe the evening traffic as if through a reddish brown filter which softens and mutes the sights and sounds of the crowded streets. The atmosphere is tranquil, and standing on the long bridge over the Niger River, with cars passing just a few feet behind you, you might look at a lone fisherman in his graceful canoe and feel that only the lovely melodies of the harp-like *kora* could capture and convey the unity of the scene. At night the temperature drops until you might wonder why you ever thought

you missed winter, and if by chance you found yourself in an isolated village at the right time and you looked up at the multitude of stars, you might hear the music of xylophones through the crisp air and believe that the clarity of the music was perhaps more than superficially appropriate to the stillness of the night.[25]

Consider finally an example from Lévi-Strauss's *Tristes tropiques*, "which, though it is very far from being a great anthropology book, or even an especially good one, is surely one of the finest books ever written by an anthropologist."[26] The example is an exegesis on the South American equivalent of bad sauce.

There had been no rain for five months and all the game had vanished. We were lucky if we managed to shoot an emaciated parrot or capture a large *tupinambis* lizard to boil in our rice, or managed to roast in their shells a land tortoise or an armadillo with black, oily flesh. More often than not, we had to be content with *xarque*, the same dried meat prepared months previously by a butcher in Cuiaba and the thick worm-infested layers of which we unrolled every morning in the sun, in order to make them less noxious, although they were usually in the same state the next day. Once, however, someone killed a wild pig; its lightly cooked flesh seemed to us more intoxicating than wine: each of us devoured more than a pound of it, and at that moment I understood the alleged gluttony of savages, which is mentioned by so many travellers as proof of their uncouthness. One only had to share their diet to experience similar pangs of hunger; to eat one's fill in such circumstances produces not merely a feeling of repletion but a positve sensation of bliss.[27]

These examples are only a slice of the life that lives in the tasteful ethnographies of Agee, Chernoff, and Lévi-Strauss. In all the examples, the writers season their prose with the non-theoretical senses to evoke a world. Agee masterfully uses a melange of smells to evoke the habitus of southern tenant farmers—their fatty diet, their filthy clothes, their stuffy houses, their abject misery. In one smelly paragraph we have a memorable portrait of the lives of these people. Chernoff records the interpenetration of sound and sight in African social life. This paragraph evokes an African world in which "participatory" music gives shape to a people's system of values as well as to their manner of living-in-the-world. With Lévi-Strauss we come back to the sensual notion of taste. In one vivid paragraph he ruminates on the link between deprivation of diet and gluttony in the Amazon. Even European intellectuals can descend into gluttony!

Should this kind of writing be excised from the ethnographic manuscripts of the future? Aren't expositions on odors, sounds, and tastes extraneous to the ethnographic message? What can these details reveal about a sociocultural system? In terms of systematic analysis, these kinds of evocative details do not uncover a system of kinship or exchange or symbolism;

hence Geertz's critique of *Tristes tropiques* as not even a good anthropology book. Tasteful anthropology books are analytic, theoretical, and ephemeral; tasteful ethnographies are descriptive, non-theoretical, and memorable. Writers of tasteful ethnographies mix an assortment of ingredients—dialogue, description, metaphor, metonomy, synecdoche, irony, smells, sights, and sounds—to create a narrative that savors the world of the Other. And just as Chernoff's drumming in Ghana once inspired members of an audience to say: "'Oh, the way you played! It moved me. It was sweet,'" so a well constructed narrative moves the listener or the reader to say: "Can I tell you a terrific story?" Indeed, there is life in the words of a good story; there is life in the prose of a tasteful ethnography.

In his monumental essay *L'Oeil et l'esprit*, Merleau-Ponty states that we lose much of the substance of life-in-the-world by thinking operationally, by defining rather than experiencing the reality of things.

> Science manipulates things and gives up living in them. It makes its own limited models of things; operating upon these indices or variables to effect whatever transformations are permitted by their definition; it comes face to face with the real world only at rare intervals. Science is and always has been that admirably active, ingenious, and bold way of thinking whose fundamental bias is to treat everything as though it were an object-in- general—as though it meant nothing to us and yet was predestined for our own use.[28]

An ethnographic discourse that "comes face to face with the real world only at rare intervals" is usually so turgid that it is digestible by only a few dedicated specialists—a discourse that will soon be forgotten. A tasteful ethnographic discourse that takes the notion of melange as its foundation would encourage writers to blend the ingredients of a world so that bad sauces might be transformed into delicious prose.

ONE MONTH OF BAD SAUCE AMONG THE SONGHAY

Stoller returned to Songhay and Adamu Jenitongo's compound in June of 1987. Jamilla had died in 1985, having drowned in a garbage pit filled with water after a torrential rain. Soon thereafter Djebo was pregnant with Hamadu, who in 1987 was about 18 months old.

In 1984 Moussa, Adamu Jenitongo's elder son, worked as a tailor; his atelier was in his father's compound. But business was slack because the Jenitongo compound was far from the center of Tillaberi. In 1985 he found a suitable atelier in Baghdad, a bustling section of Tillaberi. Moussa would leave his father's compound early in the morning, return for lunch, and leave again to complete the afternoon tasks at his tailor shop. Since he soon had more work than he could handle himself, he hired an apprentice.

By the time Stoller arrived in June of 1987, Moussa was spending much of his time at his tailor shop. He took his lunches there; for dinner, he sometimes ate small meals at the Baghdad bars: steak and french fries, green beans, omelettes. After Stoller's arrival, to fulfill the requirements of Songhay hospitality, Moussa made sure to return home to eat his meals.

The quality of the sauces hadn't changed. Djebo did not serve *fukko hoy*, but on occasion she refused to prepare meals, forcing Moussa, Stoller, and Adamu Jenitongo to eat meals of bread and sardines in soy oil.

"Things are better now that you have come," Moussa told Stoller. "Weeks go by and she doesn't prepare meals. Baba is old; he needs to eat better, but she doesn't care. My brother Moru doesn't care. And Baba, he chews kola and tobacco."

"Bad sauces are better than no sauces," Stoller said.

After one week of sauces the quality of which ranged from mediocre to bad, Stoller suffered a violent case of diarrhea. He quickly lost weight. Moussa suggested an alternative.

"Let's eat our lunches with Madame. She is an excellent cook." Madame was the daughter of Adamu Jenitongo's sister, Kedibo.

Moussa and Stoller began to eat lunch at Madame's house. The sauces were tasty: fine gombo, sesame, and squash sauces all of which were spiced delicately with permutations of garlic, ginger, locust bean, and hot pepper. Moussa and Stoller stuffed themselves, knowing that the evening fare would be much worse: tasteless rice paste drowned with watery tomato sauces all of which were spiced without imagination. There was millet in the compound, but Djebo refused to prepare it.

When it became apparent that Stoller was taking his meals at Madame's house, Djebo protested. Jemma, Djebo's mother-in-law, scowled.

"Why do you insist on your European sauces?" Jemma asked him. "Why don't you eat the sauces we prepare for you?"

Stoller did not respond directly; rather, he forced himself to eat two meals at lunch and one at dinner. Even with this increased consumption, Stoller lost more weight. His diarrhea continued.

Shamed by the bad sauces in his concession, Moussa confronted his younger brother Moru before an audience of visitors to the compound.

"How can anyone live in this compound with your lazy wife, who, when she lowers herself to prepare food for us, produces sauces that our chickens won't eat."

"Now hold on, older brother. How can you . . ."

"Shut up, you ignorant peasant. I feel like a stranger in my own home. Why return to a place where I'm not wanted?"

Moru wagged his forefinger at Moussa. "You donkey. Worthless person. Come closer and insult my wife. I'll tear your eyes out. A man who doesn't even have a wife deserves to eat shit."

"Better to be single than to be a slave to a bitch," Moussa retorted. "I'll eat my sauces elsewhere."

Moru's wife and mother restrained him.

Stoller restrained Moussa.

Adamu Jenitongo called for peace. "We shame ourselves in front of strangers."

*   *   *

Moru and Moussa are half-brothers. In the Songhay language they are *bab'izey*, which has two translations: "half-brothers" and "rivals." In Songhay *bab'izey* frequently have relationships the major ingredient of which is jealousy and bad feelings built up over a lifetime. This problem has poisoned the relationships between Moru and Moussa. As men, they have very different kinds of temperaments. Moru is hot-headed and prone to verbal and even physical confrontation. Moussa is even-tempered and keeps his emotions more to himself. Moru is a musician who sometimes works as a laborer. Moussa is a tailor who works steadily. To add more salt to an open wound, both Moussa and Moru covet the powerful secrets of their father, one of the most powerful sorcerers (*sohanci*) in Niger.

In his old age Sohanci Adamu Jenitongo hinted that he would pass on his secrets to both Moussa and Moru. But only one of them would receive his chain of power and his sacred rings. To Moru, Jemma, and Djebo, the alliance of the younger son, it was painfully obvious that Adamu Jenitongo had chosen his eldest son Moussa to succeed him. Moussa had the relatively calm disposition required for receiving great power. Moussa also had powerful allies: Kedibo, Adamu Jenitongo's youngest sister, favored Moussa because Moussa's mother, Hadjo, was the sister of her late husband. Each time she visited her brother, Kedibo extolled the virtues of her "nephew."

Moussa's steady disposition and his strategic position in the family kinship network made Moru's situation hopeless. Being powerless to change the course of events, Moru, Djebo, and Jemma chose to make life miserable for Moussa, his mother Hadjo, and Adamu Jenitongo. As the recipient of power, Moussa would soon reap considerable social rewards. He would soon become the sohanci of Tillaberi; people would fear and respect him. Moru wanted the fear and respect that his older brother was soon to receive. Powerless, Moru, Jemma, and Djebo used sauce to express their frustrations. Moussa must eat bad sauces and suffer in exchange for his good fortune.

Sauce had again become the major ingredient in the stew of (Songhay) social relations, something which Montaigne had realized long before Djebo had produced her first (though certainly not her last) bowl of *fukko hoy*.

PART II

Visions in the Field

The empiricist . . . thinks he believes what he sees, but he is much better at believing than at seeing.

Santayana

2 | *Eye, Mind, and Word in Anthropology*

Nature is on the inside.

Cézanne

To know nature is to know the texture of inner space, for, as Merleau-Ponty wrote, "quality, light, color, and depth which are there before us are there only because they awaken an echo in our body and because the body welcomes them."[1]

Cézanne and his admirer Merleau-Ponty were heretics. They dared to challenge the Aristotelian premise that nature is on the outside. How can we know if we cannot see, touch, or smell the phenomenon? How can we know if we cannot test experimentally that which we observe? How can we know if we do not have a theoretical orientation which gives form and substance to brute experiential data? Despite their intellectual heresy, Cézanne and Merleau-Ponty realized that the world consists of much more than observed objective reality and the hypotheses, theorems, and laws which scientists extract from their observations.

As mentioned earlier, Merleau-Ponty believed that we lose much of the substance of life-in-the-world by thinking operationally, by defining rather than experiencing the reality of things. Despite the hegemony of science in Western thought, Merleau-Ponty did not despair, for he envisaged the painter as the pathfinder on the road back to what he called the "there is." The painter, Merleau-Ponty writes, appreciates the life that resides in objects. The painter recognizes forces the "reverberations" of which can create sentiments in the eye and mind of the person who experiences the world.[2]

Figure 3: Gazing at space in Mehanna

But how can the painter lead us to a vantage from which we can appreciate more profoundly the life which resides in objects or in other people? For Cézanne, Merleau-Ponty, and others, painters are pathfinders to the "there is" because they give their bodies to the world. For the painter there is no Cartesian distinction between subjective data gathering and objective data analysis. "Indeed, we cannot imagine how a mind could paint. It is by lending his body to the world that the artist changes the world into paintings."[3]

And so, in the act of painting we have a metaphor for seeing and thinking in the world, a seeing-thinking from the inside. As Klee has written:

> In a forest I have felt many times over that it was not I who looked at the forest. Some days I felt that the trees were looking at me. I was there, listening.... I think the painter must be penetrated by the universe and not penetrate it.... I expect to be inwardly submerged, buried. Perhaps I paint to break out.[4]

If anthropologists take a sensual turn, they, too, can "open up." Unlike painters, we are not necessarily submerged under an avalanche of brute data which penetrate our senses; rather, we are buried under the sediment of centuries of cultural empiricism—our senses penetrate brute data. Ours is the "gaze," to borrow the apt term of Michel Foucault, of empiricism. "Gaze" is the act of seeing; it is an act of selective perception.[5] Much of what we see is shaped by our experiences, and our "gaze" has a direct bearing on what we think. And what we see and think, to take the process one step further, has a bearing upon what we say and what and how we write.

Like all human beings, anthropologists engage in the act of seeing. What differentiates anthropological seeing from other forms of seeing is that our "gaze" is directed toward an ethnographic other. We talk to ethnographic others during fieldwork and attempt to make sense of what they say and do. Due to the centrality of fieldwork to the ethnographic enterprise, most anthropologists give their eyes and minds to the world of the other. Although anthropologists, like painters, lend their bodies to the world, we tend to allow our senses to penetrate the other's world rather than letting our senses be penetrated by the world of the other. The result of this tendency is that we represent the other's world in a generally turgid discourse which often bears little resemblance to the world we are attempting to describe.

The problem of anthropological representation meets its greatest test, however, in studies of shamanism, magic, and sorcery. In these kinds of studies, social theories—the seeping sap of the turgid discourse—may be of little aid in our assessment of brute data in which the "irrationalities" of, say, a magical vision play a major role. Anthropologists engaged in the study of shamanism, for example, may observe or experience something so extraordinary that they can find no reasonable explanation for it. How do we represent these data? Should we include them in our discourse? What would the painter do?

Those anthropologists who have observed or experienced something which is beyond the edge of rationality tend to discuss it in informal settings—over lunch, dinner, or a drink. Serious anthropological discussion of the extraordinary, in fact, transcends the bar or restaurant only on rare occasions.[6] In formal settings we are supposed to be dispassionate analysts; we are not supposed to include in discourse our confrontations with the extraordinary because they are unscientific. It is simply not appropriate to expose to our colleagues the texture of our hearts and the uncertainties of our "gaze." Many French anthropologists have lambasted Jeanne Favret-Saada for her published study of witchcraft in the Bocage of Western France, in which she reveals what it means to be personally enmeshed in a system of magic-sorcery. In her first book, *Deadly Words*, Favret-Saada questions the Cartesian foundation of the epistemology of anthropology. In *Corps pour corps*, her second book (co-authored with Josée Contreras), she journeys beyond the boundary of criticism and becomes a "pathfinder," for in this text, a journal of her fieldwork, she experiments with the form of anthropological discourse.

The painter "sees what inadequacies keep the world from being a painting . . . and sees painting as an answer to all these inadequacies."[7] What of the inadequacies of anthropological discourse? In the remainder of this chapter, by way of an epistemological discussion of my experience as an apprentice to sorcerers among the Songhay of Niger, I argue that we need to transform ourselves from ethnographic "spectators into seers."[8] Although the account of my exposure to the mysteries of the world of Songhay sorcery is necessarily personal, I hope that the reader will grasp the epistemological utility of so vivid an account of field experience. If we learn to "read" and "write" in a manner similar to the way the painter paints, we may well be able to sensualize prose which represents others so that our books become the study of human being as well as human behavior.[9]

JOURNEY INTO SONGHAY INNER SPACE

My journey into Songhay inner space[10] began innocently enough in 1976 in the village of Mehanna, a cluster of mudbrick compounds divided into seven neighborhoods, which hugs the west bank of the Niger River in the Republic of Niger. I had been in Mehanna investigating how Songhay use symbolic forms in local level politics, the topic of my doctoral research. During my first few months in Mehanna much of my time was spent tape-recording formal and informal orations which occurred during public rituals or private discussion groups.[11] Soon after I had moved into my house in Mehanna, a two-room mudbrick structure in the neighborhood of nobles, I noticed, between the beams of my roof, a bird's nest made of dried mud. Two small birds, one white and one black, would periodically enter and leave the nest, and I suspected that soon there would be more than two in my house. My discovery became all the more annoying when I observed that the birds had defecated on my dirt floor. Despite the rustic nature of my mudbrick and dirt surroundings, I tried to maintain my admittedly ethnocentric standards of cleanliness. Disgusted with the slovenly habits of these birds, I knocked down their nest. The birds decided to test my perseverance, however; they came back and built another nest, only to be destroyed. They returned; I destroyed; they returned; I destroyed; and so on. Finally, I surrendered, helplessly acquiescing to the birds' continuing residence, their intermittent defecation on my floor, my tables, my books, and even my plates and pans! My view after six months of battle was: Hell, if they defecate on my plates, I'll simply wash them.

This attitude toward the filthy presence of the birds in my house was, I suppose, part of my Songhayization. Soon, I simply regarded the two birds as permanent fixtures in my house and came to ignore them. One afternoon, however, while I was typing my fieldnotes of the day in the presence of Djibo, a farmer from the village, one, maybe both, of the birds defecated on my head.

"Birdshit! Goddam country. Goddam village. Goddam village!" I screamed in English as I jumped off my chair and kicked the floor of my house.

"Praise be to God," Djibo chanted loudly, raising his hands skyward.

"How can you say something like that at a time like this!" I snapped.

"I'm not laughing at you, Paul, I feel joy in my heart."

"Joy! What joy can there be in this?"

"Yes, joy. I have seen something today."

"No kidding."

"Yes, I have seen a sign. You see, Paul, I am a sorko. My father is a sorko. And my grandfather, and grandfather's grandfather—all have been sorkos."

"What does that have to do with me?" Despite my frustration I was intrigued, for I had heard and read about the powers of the sorko, one of three kinds of Songhay magician-healers.

"Until today, my being a sorko had nothing to do with you," Djibo continued, "but today I have seen a sign. You have been pointed out to me. Yes, I am a sorko and now that you have been pointed out to me, I want you to come to my compound tomorrow after the evening prayer so that we might begin to learn texts."

"What are you talking about?"

"I am saying that I want you to learn to be a sorko," Djibo said as he cracked his knuckles. "The choice is yours to make. If you choose my path, come to my compound tomorrow." Djibo walked toward the door, stopped at the threshold and looked back toward me. "Praise be to God."

My immediate inclination was to wonder: But what would the members of my dissertation committee think? . . . I would like to study with you, but I really must complete my dissertation work. My second inclination was to accept this rare invitation because I knew that this kind of opportunity could not be deferred.

Learning to be a Sorko

The sorko in Songhay society is a praise-singer to the spirits of the Songhay pantheon, and a healer who treats cases of witchcraft, sorcery, and spirit sickness. Most sorkos are the patrilineal descendants of Faran Maka Bote, the first sorko, the son of the fisherman Nisili Bote and a river genie, Maka. How could I, an American, fit into the sorko's genealogy? Through my study of ritual texts I soon learned that there are two categories of sorko: lineal descendants of Faran Maka Bote, and people like me who are trained and initiated because a practicing sorko sees a sign. The latter category is called *sorko benya* (lit. "slaves of the sorko"). People in this category learn almost as much as lineal descendants, but there are some secrets that a master will impart only to consanguineal kin.

The novice sorko must memorize scores of ritual incantations, learn how to find special herbal ingredients, and then learn how to mix them correctly into potions.[12] When the potion is prepared and administered to a client, the apprentice must learn how to recite the appropriate ritual text. Once a novice is selected, he is said to have "entered into *sorkotarey*." When I entered into sorkotarey, Djibo said:

"You know nothing. Listen, remember, and learn."

This I did until I was ready to be initiated by Djibo's father, Mounmouni Koda, who, after more than fifty years of study and reflection, had become a master sorko.

A person becomes a master sorko only when, after years of apprenticeship, he hears from his dying father (or initiator) the most powerful secrets. Armed with this knowledge, the new master takes upon his shoulders the spiritual burden of his community to protect it from the forces of evil: witchcraft, sorcerers, and the force of maliferous spirits. Mounmouni Koda, a short old man with penetrating black eyes and a quiet laugh, listened to my recitation of ritual texts and spirit praise-songs. Satisfied, he consented to initiate me as a sorko benya. He prepared a special food, called in Songhay *kusu*, and told me that when I met other people along the path (of sorkotarey) I should tell them that I am "full," or that I should push my forefinger into my stomach. He also told me that the learning never stops.

"Your journey into the world of magic [what I am here calling Songhay inner space] will end only with your death."

Because I still knew "nothing" about sorkotarey, my initiator, the now deceased sorko, sent me to "sit" with a great master healer of the Songhay, Sohanci Adamu Jenitongo, a patrilineal descendant of the great "Magic King" of the Songhay Empire, Sonni Ali Ber. During my stay with Adamu Jenitongo, we would talk about the Songhay universe. He would never lecture me; rather, he insisted that I ask questions and, if the questions were well formed, he might provide an answer to them. If the questions, which were often about obscure ritual texts, were not well formed, he would ask me to think more about the texts.

From this frail old man I learned scores of ritual texts designed to protect me from the forces of evil which I would confront on the path of sorkotarey.

"And if a witch or sorcerer should ever attack you," he told me, "you must recite the *genji how*," a text with the power to harmonize the forces of the bush.

Studies with Sohanci Adamu Jenitongo capped my year of doctoral fieldwork. I returned to the United States committed to completing my study on the use of symbolic forms in Songhay local-level politics, and so I completed my dissertation. My incipient training as a sorko benya, however, had convinced me of the depth of my ignorance about Songhay cosmology, magic, sorcery, and witchcraft, and I was determined to continue along my path. I was by no means a believer. I simply wanted to explore every opportunity to continue my studies with Adamu Jenitongo. My view of Songhay sorcery up to that point had been conditioned by my scientific gaze. I sought explanations for the phenomena I had observed. Many of the healings I had witnessed and participated in could be explained, or so I reasoned, through a detailed pharmacological study of the curative agents in the various plants which the healer administered to his patients. I made notes of the kinds of plants used in potions and categorized them scientifically. I also analyzed the significance of the ritual texts I was learning from a structuralist perspective, teasing out of them meaningful oppositions. During a visit in 1979, Adamu Jenitongo encouraged me to write down the incantations and the names of plants, but he cautioned me never to publish the incantations in the original Songhay; for as he said: "It is in the sound of the incantation that the power is carried."

I was unconvinced. How could words carry power? How could words have an existence of their own—a far cry from the Western conception that words are neutral instruments of reference? Despite my commitment to learning about Songhay sorcery from the Songhay perspective—from the inside, to borrow Roger Bastide's notion—Adamu Jenitongo sensed my growing skepticism.

"It is time for you to travel," he told me. "Go to Wanzerbé and seek out a woman called Kassey. She will teach you a great deal about the Songhay world of magic."

Crossing the Threshold in Wanzerbé

I did not arrive in Wanzerbé until the middle of the night, thanks to having been stuck in the sand twice during the trip. On the first occasion, we freed ourselves easily. The second time proved to be more difficult; it took all the passengers more than an hour to dislodge the tires of the Land Rover from the soft dune sand.

Djibril, our driver, dropped us off at the center of Wanzerbé. The space was deserted but for one man who sat in front of his dry-goods store. Idrissa, my friend, called to him, "Hassane, come."

Hassane's shaved head gleamed in the full moonlight. He carried one of the two sacks of rice to the compound of Idrissa's family in Karia (one of the two quarters of Wanzerbé). Idrissa carried the other one. Trudging through the thick sand of the path, we were soon at the compound, in which no person stirred. The compound, an ellipse of thirty mudbrick houses, looked the same as it had during my last visit. Idrissa knocked on the door of his father's house. "Baba, it's Idrissa."

Koundiababa, Idrissa's father, opened the door. He squinted at us. "Idrissa?"

Idrissa asked his father for lodging. He gave us the house next to his own, since its usual occupant, Mamadu, was away in the Ivory Coast earning money to supplement the family's income. Idrissa found some blankets, and we bedded down for the night.

Kassey, Idrissa's stepmother and the person whom I had come to see, was not in Wanzerbé and would not return for three weeks. Idrissa recommended that I visit Dunguri, Kassey's associate. I agreed.

We walked down a sandy embankment toward the road that separated the two neighborhoods in Wanzerbé. The space between the two neighborhoods contained empty market stalls. Just beyond them stood the minareted Friday mosque. We plodded along sandy paths between low walls of compounds. We greeted women who were pounding millet in their mortars. Once in the quarter of Sohanci, we encountered many of Idrissa's people from his mother's side. They greeted us and asked after our health. Next to the small neighborhood mosque in the center of Sohanci was a clearing with a free-standing thatched canopy in the center. A dozen older men reclined in the shade of that roof. We greeted them and asked them not to get up to shake our hands. They did not. Finally, we reached Dunguri's compound, which had no walls. Dunguri's house was squeezed between two large granaries and a mudbrick corral for calves.

Idrissa clapped three times outside the door of the woman's house. She came out and hugged him. As she greeted Idrissa, she glanced at me. "Who is this stranger?" she asked Idrissa.

"This stranger," I interjected in Songhay, "is Paul from America. I am Idrissa's friend."

"Idrissa, come into my house. We should talk. You, too, can come in, stranger."

We stepped down into Dunguri's house. Bright cotton blankets covered her whitewashed walls. She had draped a score of additional blankets over two beds which had been placed at either end of the rectangular room. She gave us metal folding chairs to sit on. She, too, sat down on a hardbacked chair, but eschewed its support as she leaned forward with her hands on her knees.

Idrissa and Dunguri discussed the health and sickness of the people they knew. So-and-so's son was in Niamey serving in the army. So-and-so's daughter had married and was living in a neighboring village. Amadu had not been well lately. He had gone off to Tera for medical attention, but the

Guinea worm still made him suffer. And an older man had recently died from liver disease. Idrissa asked Dunguri about the harvest.

"It was good, Idrissa. My slave [husband] worked hard and brought in three hundred bundles of millet."

"Our harvest in Mehanna," Idrissa told her, "was not good."

Dunguri nodded. "Some years we are blessed and in other years we are cursed. A town like Tegey only ten kilometers from here—Tegey might have a good harvest while we here may not harvest one bundle of millet."

During the conversation Dunguri ignored me: she did not look at me even once. Coming from someone else I would have deemed the behavior rude; from a Songhay it was most peculiar. In most circumstances Songhay are hospitable, and they are curious about the ways of strangers—not so this woman Dunguri. I sat impatiently as they conversed, taking the opportunity to study her face. I would never have guessed that this small plump woman was a priestess. Her puffy face did not look particularly intelligent, nor did her gaze seem forceful. Suddenly I heard the word "stranger." Dunguri was asking Idrissa about me. This woman had the audacity to ask Idrissa about my work when I was present in the room. I remained silent, though, as Idrissa crudely outlined my work in Mehanna and Tillaberi. He told her I was writing a book.

"He will not be using a machine to shoot film, will he?"

Idrissa assured her I had no interest in film.

She turned toward me. "Stranger, where did you get your rings? They are very beautiful."

Adamu Jenitongo had warned me never to reveal to anyone the true nature of the rings that he had given me for protection. "Thank you," I said to Dunguri. "I just bought these rings in Ayoru. I like Tuareg rings very much."

Dunguri addressed Idrissa. "Show the stranger my granaries and animals. I have no more time to talk with him today." She stood up, stepped out of her house, and walked into her compound.

Idrissa and I looked at one another. Never had I been treated so ungraciously by a Songhay host. Idrissa frowned and muttered something about Dunguri's recent sufferings and suggested we look at her granaries and animals. When we stepped into the compound, we saw no one. The granary was filled with millet, and Dunguri, unlike most of her neighbors in Sohanci, possessed a small herd of cows and calves, a sign of wealth.

"She lives better than the others, does she not, Idrissa?"

"Yes," he agreed. "She is a zima and a powerful magician. She is well paid for her services."

Tired and frustrated, I prepared for bed. What was the sense of my coming to Wanzerbé? I couldn't wait three weeks for the elusive Kassey.

And why had the woman Dunguri been so abrupt with me? I longed to return to Tillaberi or to Niamey. I longed for home. But I had to remain in Wanzerbé for at least one week, because there were no trucks going to Ayoru until Saturday, the day before the market. My kerosene lantern flickered out, I reconciled myself to spending some time in that God-forsaken place, and I slipped into sleep.

Some time later I awoke to the tattoo of steps on the roof of the house. Suddenly I had the strong impression that something had entered the house. I felt its presence and I was frightened. Set to abandon the house to whatever hovered in the darkness, I started to roll off my mat. But my lower body did not budge. I pinched my leaden thighs and felt nothing. My heart raced. I couldn't flee. What could I do to save myself? As a sorko benya, I began to recite the genji how, for Adamu Jenitongo had told me that if I ever felt danger I should recite this incantation until I had conquered my fear. And so I recited and recited and recited until I began to feel a slight tingling in my hips. Encouraged, I continued to recite the incantation, and the tingling spread down my thighs to my legs. My voice cracked, but I continued to recite. Slowly, the tingling spread from my legs to my feet. I pinched my thigh—it hurt—and tested my response along the length of my legs. Gingerly, I rolled off the mat and stood up. The presence had left the room. Exhausted, I lay back on my straw mat and fell into a deep sleep.

The next morning Idrissa woke me. I got up slowly and told Idrissa that I was going to visit Dunguri.

"I'll come with you."

"No, Idrissa. I must go alone."

I cannot explain why I felt obliged to confront Dunguri, for I was certain that it was she who had precipitated the paralysis in my legs. The previous night I had reacted to my crisis like a sorcerer and, having weathered the crisis, I had to continue to behave like a Songhay sorcerer. And so I slowly walked out of my compound in Karia. The sun was still low in the eastern sky and the air was cool and dry. But I was tired; my heart pounded against my chest and I wondered what might happen when I confronted Dunguri. I walked past the compound of Kassey and saw no one inside. I climbed up the small dune upon which was situated the quarter of Sohanci. An old man in a tattered white robe greeted me in Songhay but, seeing my eyes, told me to continue. As I neared the top of the dune I saw Dunguri's compound ahead. The air was still, and I froze to the spot. Then I remembered what Adamu Jenitongo once told me: When a man on the path reaches the fork in the road, he must make his choice of direction and continue forward. And so I did. With trembling arms and wobbling knees I entered Dunguri's compound and stood in its center, waiting. After what seemed to me a very long time, Dunguri emerged from her house. She stared at me, and I tried to conceal my nervousness. But then she smiled at me and approached, her pace quickening. I was fixed in place by my own apprehension. As she closed the distance between us, I saw that she was beaming. Stopping a few feet from me, she said: "Now I know that you are a man with a pure heart." She took my left hand and placed it in hers. "You are ready. Come into my house and we shall begin to learn."

REPRESENTATION AND ETHNOGRAPHIC REALISM

The description of my encounter with Dunguri ends here, even though I have seen her since that meeting which thrust me for the first time into the magical dimension of the Songhay world. This account, however, is more than a personal narrative; it is an event-in-the-field that forces us to confront some serious epistemological questions about the nature of anthropology and what it represents. Is it appropriate to include in anthropological discourse such a personal, bizarre, and sensuous account? My first inclination was to answer this question with an emphatic "No!" Indeed, in my first article about some of my experiences in the world of Songhay sorcery, I scrupulously avoided mentioning the fact that much of what I had learned about Songhay sorcery had been from the "inside" as an initiated apprentice. In that text I alluded to my involvement only in a footnote describing how a healer in the village of Mehanna came to accept me as his student.[13] Why did I edit myself out of this earlier text? The answer is simple: we do not usually write what we want to write. In my case, I had conformed to one of the conventions of ethnographic realism, according to which the author should be unintrusive in an ethnographic text.[14] As Foucault has powerfully demonstrated, all discourse is shaped by standards of acceptability—the episteme—which govern the appropriateness of (ethnographic) content and style.[15] These standards of acceptability, moreover, determine both how an author will construct a text and which kinds of texts are ultimately published.[16]

Stylistic evidence of these standards of acceptability, these conventions of representation, emerges from the most cursory examination of wide-ranging varieties of discourse. In the eighteenth-century novel, for example, we have the picaresque convention in which authors open their texts with statements concerning their family pedigree as well as their lust for travel.[17] The important point here is that these conventions of representation are not limited to novels by Swift, Defoe, and Sterne, but permeate works of non-fiction as well. We see what Pratt calls the "monarch-of-all-I-see convention" in such diverse works as Richard F. Burton's *The Lake Regions of Central Africa*, Alberto Moravia's *Which Tribe Do You Belong To?*, or Paul Theroux's *The Old Patagonian Express*. In all these texts the authors describe scenes from a masterly metaphoric balcony overlooking a vast panorama. Consider an example from Moravia:

> From the balcony of my room I had a panoramic view over Accra, capital of Ghana. Beneath a sky of hazy blue, filled with mists and ragged yellow and grey clouds, the town looked like a thick, dark cabbage soup in which numerous pieces of white pasta were on the boil. The cabbages were tropical trees with rich, trailing, heavy foliage of dark green speckled with black shadows; the pieces of pasta the brand new buildings of reinforced concrete, numbers of which were now rising all over the town.[18]

Here, Moravia objectifies and perhaps trivializes the city of Accra, using such bizarre European imagery as "cabbage soup" and "pasta." In the end Pratt warns us that scholars must be sensitive to the messages which are hidden in our taken-for-granted conventions of representation, and criticizes "discourses that implicitly or explicitly dehumanize, trivialize, or devalue other realities in the name of Western superiority."[19] Anthropologists should especially take heed of Pratt's warning, for, like other scholars, we, too, have a tacit set of conventions (ethnographic realism) which govern most of what and how we represent the ethnographic other.

Conventions of Representation in Ethnographic Realism

Chapter 1 summarized Marcus and Cushman's description of the impact of ethnographic realism on anthropological discourse.[20]

Contrary to those comments, however, the source of ethnographic realism must actually be sought prior to the establishment of anthropology as an academic discipline and the establishment of fieldwork as the methodological foundation of ethnographic works. Indeed, ethnographic realism flows nicely into the stream of the Western epistemological tradition which Whitehead characterizes as a "series of footnotes to Plato."[21]

Plato emerges at a time in Greek thinking, of course, when there was a perceived need for systematic reflection, a need to create patterned order from the chaos of continuous flux. From the fragments of flux, to paraphrase Richard Rorty, Plato devises the notion of the search for Truth, in which we turn away from subjective involvement to objectivity.[22] Plato's quest for Truth (or Forms) through objectivity was his solution to the puzzle of the infinite variability to be found in the world of appearances. And so, Plato becomes the first thinker to distinguish appearance from reality. Behind every appearance, he tells us, there is a hidden immutable Form. These Forms become the archetypes of knowledge, which must be distinguished from opinion. Opinions, in Plato's view, are as unstable as the flux of appearances. Knowledge, on the other hand, is an immutable pillar of reality.

From these relatively simple distinctions, the epistemology of Western philosophic tradition is born. These metaphysical distinctions have not been disputed; rather, thinkers since Plato have disputed the question of how we discover the reality (the One) hidden behind appearances (the Many), how we arrive at Truth.

As Whitehead suggests, the search for the One in the Many has been at the heart of Western scholarly discourse. This search has directed the thinking of such diverse groups of thinkers as the scholastic philosophers, the romantics, the structuralists, the linguists, and the Marxists. Saussure, for example, considers *parole* beyond his focus of study, for it is so hetero-geneous that "We cannot put it into any category of human facts, and we cannot discover its unity."[23] In his monumental work, *The Elementary Structures of Kinship*, Lévi-Strauss demonstrates that to discover the mean-ing of a given institution, like marriage, we must commit ourselves to an analysis which uncovers the reality obscured by the haze of appearances. In the end, Lévi-Strauss argues that "it is exchange, always exchange, that emerges as the fundamental and common basis of *all* modalities of the institution of marriage" (emphasis added).[24] The tradition of the search for the One in the Many leads ultimately to the dissolution of man in which "ethnographic analysis tries to arrive at invariants beyond the empirical diversity of societies."[25] Ethnographic realism lends itself to this aged tradition, for it, too, seeks the One in the Many; from bits and pieces of data, realist ethnographies attempt to "evoke a social and cultural unity."[26]

Ethnographic realism, as it is described by Marcus and Cushman, manifests itself as a set of conventions, which have already been described in Chapter 1. To reiterate briefly, these conventions produce ethnographies which claim to depict the total ethnographic picture of a society. In these ethnographies, the people have little or no voice in what is usually third person narrative filled with anthropological jargon.

The conventions of ethnographic realism have had a varied impact on the quality of writing in ethnographies. Many of the early realist ethnogra-phies are magnificently written. Some of the passages in Firth's *We, the Tikopia,* are poetic, especially at the beginning of the text:

> In the cool of the morning, just before sunrise, the bow of the *Southern Cross* headed towards the eastern horizon, on which a tiny blue outline was faintly visible. Slowly it grew into a rugged mountain mass, standing up sheer from the ocean; then as we approached within a few miles it revealed around its base a narrow ring of low, flat land thick with vegetation. The sullen grey day with its lowering clouds strengthened my grim impression of a solitary peak, wild and stormy, upthrust in a waste of waters.[27]

Since Firth's mission was to depict the total culture of the Tikopia, he was blessed with a descriptive license which few anthropologists or editors would tolerate today. In today's climate the styles of ethnographic texts are much more circumscribed. Take the beginning of Feld's excellent ethnography of sound in Kaluli society: "This is an ethnographic study of sound as a cultural system. . . . My intention is to show how an analysis of modes and codes of sound communication leads to an understanding of the ethos and quality of life in . . . society."[28] With very few exceptions, anthropological writing has become as flat, neutral, and sludgy as the prose of the natural sciences, as anthropologists have attempted to legitimize the scientific nature of their discipline.

Experiments in Anthropological Discourse

Hundreds of anthropologists now worry about the philosophical and political implications of the conventions of representation associated with ethnographic realism. Recent concerns with the accurate representation of the native point of view, and the relationship of anthropologist and other, have resulted in the publication of a number of experimental "reflexive" ethnographies. In these experimental texts, the authors tend to focus on differences between the anthropologist and the other.[29] "So even if the writers of these texts must rely on a culturally biased language of description, they strive to make cultural difference a key goal of textual construction."[30] Moreover, the experimental author "offers an account of his intellectual and fieldwork experience with which readers can identify; through the writer's self-reflection as a narrative vehicle, they slide into a receptivity for descriptions that could otherwise appear implausible to them."[31]

Despite the experimentality of the newer works, most of them consider typical anthropological subjects of study, albeit through altered conventions of representation. By contrast, Favret-Saada's *Deadly Words* not only experiments with some of the conventions of ethnographic realism, but also challenges the major suppositions of the Western epistemological tradition. Alone among the narrative ethnographies (with the exception of *In Sorcery's Shadow* and *Corps pour corps*), Favret-Saada's book considers the subject of magic-sorcery; the subject, if considered from the "inside"— as it is by Favret-Saada and Stoller and Olkes—forces us to think about adopting other conventions of representation which may carry anthropology yet deeper into the being of the other. Are there other ways of writing ethnographies that better solve the problems of voice, authority, and authenticity? *What if I talk more about the people*

LANGUAGE, PAINTING, AND ANTHROPOLOGICAL STYLE

Nature continues to be on the outside in anthropological discourse, the experimental ethnographies notwithstanding. As a consequence a (poetic) journey such as mine into inner dimensions of space, sentiment, or thought is usually not considered part of an anthropological discourse. The event which I portray is perhaps described in too lyrical or literary a style. If I presented the "event" as part of a longer journal of my experience in the world of Songhay sorcery, both the form and content would today be deemed non-anthropological. In short, the style, form, and content of my text involve passions, sentiments, fears, and doubts. This is the dense discourse of literature and not the opaque discourse of anthropology.

Representation-of and Representation-as

The discourse of anthropology is characterized by representation "as," a mode of discourse in which "the sign ceases to be a form of the world; and it ceases to be bound to what it marks by solid and secret bonds of resemblance or affinity."[32] In anthropological discourse we read analyses of culture-as-a thermodynamic system, or society-as-a system, or religion-as-a mechanism of social control. Representation "of," by contrast, is the act of describing something, an act which is fundamentally creative. Nelson Goodman writes:

> Representation or description is apt, effective, illuminating, subtle, intriguing, to the extent that the artist or writer grasps fresh and significant relationships and devises means for making them manifest. Discourse or depiction that marks off familiar units and sorts them into standard sets of well worn labels may sometimes be serviceable, even if humdrum. The marking off of new elements or classes of familiar ones by labels of new kinds, or by new combinations of old labels, may provide new insight. Gombrich stresses Constable's metaphor: "Painting is a science ... of which pictures are but the experiments." In representation, the artist must make use of old habits when he wants to elicit novel objects or connections. . . .
>
> In sum, effective representation and description require invention. They are creative. They inform each other; and they form, relate, and distinguish objects. That nature imitates art is too timid a dictum. Nature is a product of art and discourse.[33]

Style and Meaning

One way to carry the reader of anthropological works into new thought-provoking worlds is not just to experiment with the representative conventions of narrative structures, but to experiment with the language of ethnography itself. This more revolutionary kind of experimentation has a long and provocative history. In the nineteenth century the styles of Nietzsche and Carlyle challenged the discourse of the classical episteme. Hartmann comments that "In Carlyle the link between language and terrorism becomes itself a form of terrorism. Like many language-combatants of the era, he uses the medium of style against classical humanism: its statuesque decorum."[34] And what can be made of the arresting styles of Joyce, of

Heidegger, or of Derrida? What do these iconoclastic styles imply for literature, for philosophy, for anthropology?

They imply a great deal. When an anthropologist is confronted with an incident that he or she cannot explain—like my paralysis in Wanzerbé—the pillars of the aged metaphysic begin to crumble; the conventions of representation that worked so beautifully in a previous study are no longer adequate. Nietzsche wrote that the mission of science

> is to make existence intelligible and thereby justified. . . . Socrates and his successors, down to our day, have considered all moral and sentimental accomplishments—noble deeds, compassion, self-sacrifice, heroism . . . to be ultimately derived from the dialectic of knowledge, and therefore teachable. . . . But science, spurred on by its energetic notions, approaches irresistibly those outer limits where the optimism of its logic must collapse. . . . When the inquirer, having pushed to the circumference, realizes how logic in that place curls about itself and bites its own tail, he is struck with a new kind of perception: a tragic perception, which requires, to make it tolerable, the remedy of art.[35]

Style, Voice, and the Indirect Language

In *The Prose of the World*, Merleau-Ponty describes the power of language—direct and indirect—to bring to life thoughts that have never been expressed before. He writes that "language leads us to things themselves to the precise extent that it *is* signification before *having* signification."[36] The "gaze" of the painter who is penetrated by the universe "appropriates correspondences, questions, and answers which, in the world, are revealed only inaudibly and always smothered in a stupor of objects."[37] The "gaze" of the writer is similar to that of the painter.

> Given the experience, which may be banal but for the writer, captures a particular savor of life, given, in addition, words, forms, phrasing, syntax, even literary genres, modes of narrative that through custom are always endowed with a common meaning—the writer's task is to choose, assemble, wield, and torment those instruments in such a way that they induce the same sentiment of life that dwells in the writer at every moment, deployed henceforth in an imaginary world and in the transparent body of language.[38]

The inaudible nature of significance in both painting and writing constitutes, for Merleau-Ponty, the "indirect language," the representation of things themselves. The "indirect language" is expressed in the painter's style or in the writer's voice. Style, voice, and the indirect language are created through the interaction of painters with their worlds, or the interaction of writers with their others. "The words, the lines, and the colors which express me come from me as my gestures are torn from me by what I want to say, the way my gestures are and by what I want to do. . . . In the art of prose, words carry the speaker and listener into a common universe by drawing both toward a new signification through their power to designate in excess of their accepted definition."[39] Stressing the importance of language in representing the world, Merleau-Ponty writes in *Le Visible et l'invisible*, about the discourse of philosophy. His comments are applicable to the discourse of anthropology:

> Words most charged with philosophy are not necessarily those that contain what they say, but rather those that most energetically open upon being, because they more closely convey the life of the whole and make our habitual evidences vibrate until they disjoin. Hence it is a question whether philosophy as the reconquest of brute and wild being can be accomplished by the resources of the eloquent language, or whether it would not be necessary for philosophy to use language in a way that takes from its power of immediate or direct signification in order to equal it with what it wishes all the same to say.[40]

Here Merleau-Ponty calls for "voice" in philosophical discourse, a new discourse in which the indirect language of the author brings the reader into contact with "brute and wild being." Let philosophers, he suggests, bring their readers into the world of "brute and wild being" in the same manner that Stendahl uses common words and events as emissaries from his world. "I create Stendahl while I am reading him. But that is because he first knew how to bring me to dwell in him."[41] The magic of discourse and communication, to summarize, is accomplished through style, voice and the "indirect language." There should be more of an emphasis on an "indirect language" in anthropology.

TEXTS, WRITERS, AND READERS

We can now return to the question of how to describe-represent my confrontation with Dunguri in the Songhay village of Wanzerbé. My initial solution was to edit myself out of the text and substitute an invisible third person narrator. What to do now? Should I, rather, describe the confrontation even more dispassionately, discuss it as one small part of Songhay witchcraft, and place the data into the broader theoretical context of witchcraft studies? Neither of these tacks is satisfactory to me, for, like it or not, there is a direct relationship between the degree of the anthropologists' subjective involvement and the forms they choose for their discourse. In *Ecstasy and Healing in Nepal*, Larry Peters describes his apprenticeship to a Tamang shaman, admitting that he had only begun to understand the existential dynamics of trance states. But Peters's book is disjointed: Part One is a representation-of his experience, which in Part Two he transforms into a psychoanalytic analysis (representation-as). Would the form of Peters's discourse be different if he had proceeded deeper into the inner dimensions of Tamang shamanism? Such a transformation of discourse is evident in the works of Jeanne Favret-Saada. In *Deadly Words* she felt the need to justify her personal involvement in the system of sorcery in the Bocage of western France. In *Corps pour corps*, together with Josée Contreras, she wrote a journal of her experience, a collage of her joys, epistemological doubts, fears, and disappointments in the field from January 1969 to December 1970. Through her "voice," Favret-Saada brings the reader into the world of the Bocage. Informants become people with distinct personalities, likes and dislikes, strengths and weaknesses, thoughts and powers of observation. The text of the Bocage—the field and the sorcery within it—opens itself up to readers and sweeps them into a very special world. Hence, the widespread success of the book among a diverse audience, ranging from intellectuals at the Sorbonne to the Bocage peasants about whom the book was written. And between the beautifully written lines of *Corps pour corps* the anthropological reader is struck by the theoretical importance of this work. But people will ask: Is the work of Favret-Saada and Contreras really anthropology?

Once the anthropological writer has experienced "the inside" or "the place where logic bites its own tail," the discourse of ethnographic realism is no longer completely adequate. When I confronted first-hand the powers of Dunguri in Wanzerbé and acted like a Songhay sorcerer, all my assumptions about the world were uprooted from their foundation in Western metaphysics. Nothing that I had learned or could learn from social theory could have prepared me for Dunguri. Once I crossed the threshold into the Songhay world of sorcery, and felt the texture of fear and the exaltation of repelling the force of a sorcerer, my view of Songhay culture could no longer be one of a structuralist, a symbolist, or a Marxist. Given my intense experience—and all field experiences are intense whether they involve trance, sorcery, or kinship—I will need in future works to seek a different mode of expression, a mode in which the event becomes the author of the text and the writer becomes the interpreter of the event who serves as an intermediary between the event (author) and the readers.

Just as painters, according to Cézanne and Klee, should allow the universe to penetrate them, anthropological writers should allow the events of the field—be they extraordinary or mundane—to penetrate them. In this way the world of the field cries out silently for description and we, as anthropological writers, are put to the task of representation-of which philosophers ranging from Goodman to Merleau-Ponty suggest is a creative act, a search for voice and "the indirect language." In this way the anthropological writer, using evocative language, brings life to the field and beckons the reader to discover something new—a new theoretical insight, a new thought, a new feeling or appreciation.

Figure 4: The Friday mosque in Mehanna

On their existential path in inner space, sorcerers, in the end, create their own sorcery; painters create their own styles. And just as writers need to spend many years searching for their own voices, so we anthropologists need to find a "voice" and create works which bring readers to dwell within us as we walk along our solitary paths in the field, exposing our hearts so full of excitement, fear, and doubt.

3 | *"Gazing" at the Space of Songhay Politics*

If anthropologists take a sensual turn they will position themselves to let the other's world penetrate their being. This repositioning, as I argued in Chapters 1 and 2, would transform the fundamental relationship among our writers, texts and readers. In most ethnographic texts, anthropologists are the authors. The texts they produce are the products of their disciplinary socialization. In more sensualized ethnographies the scenes described (people, interviews, ritual) become authors, the anthropologist becoming the intermediary between the author and an audience. These texts are then the products of socialization in two worlds. Socialization in two worlds implies a decrease of authorial control and an increase in authorial humility. Although our "gaze" plays many tricks on us in the field, we rarely acknowledge our interpretative errors in our texts. In this chapter I discuss a case in which my "gaze" led me to "see" something which did not exist.

* * *

Jean Rouch, who has learned much about the Songhay-speaking peoples of the Republic of Niger during the past forty-five years, once told me about an error in his perception of Songhay spatial patterns. Despite his great knowledge of the Songhay, he had only recently realized that Songhay roads do not intersect, but rather end in a fork with two new roads going off in different directions. "I was so used to viewing the world from my European perspective," he said, "that I saw intersections rather than forks." As we later agreed, the road-as-a-fork is a significant symbol in Songhay cosmology. If it took a truly perceptive anthropologist thirty years to discover what Whitehead called the "delusion" of his perception, what can one say about other anthropologists whose generalizations about social life are based upon one, two, or ten years of fieldwork?[1] Do anthropological analyses suffer from significant omissions generated from the "delusion" of the anthropologist's perception? Are most anthropological theories based on misconceptions stemming from the inability of the anthropologist to perceive something his or her informant takes for granted? These are haunting questions for anthropologists who in the course of fieldwork must struggle to comprehend systems of symbolic and social relations that are, for the most part, outside the scope of their experience.

In the remainder of this chapter I advocate an anthropological vision in which the scholar must not only make use of keen observational skills, but also reflect critically on his or her own philosophico-cultural biases so as to guard against seeing or writing about something that does not exist. More specifically, I argue that the deep-seated influence of post-Socratic Greek philosophy has rendered anthropology, not to mention psychology and sociology, a social science engaged in the search for the static universals of social life. This search can often delude our field perceptions, conditioning us to see things which have no importance or meaning to the people we study.

SPACE, POLITICS, AND SONGHAY SOCIETY

Songhay has a long and glorious history (see the Introduction) reaching its greatest glory under the rule of Askia Mohammed Touré in 1493–1528. During the 125-year imperial epoch there evolved a stratified society constituted of free Songhay, slaves, and tribute-paying foreigners. There are many vestiges of the imperial and precolonial past in contemporary Songhay. Nobles, the patrilineal descendants of Askia Mohammed Touré, are traditional chiefs. In many cases, descendants of former slaves are today clients to noble patrons. Foreigners no longer pay tribute to the empire, but they are still stigmatized strangers in Songhay communities.

The most striking aspect of Songhay social organization is its social exclusivity, which is maintained not only through genealogy but through social interaction. Nobles are expected to dress in white—the sartorial sign of a man who does not work with his hands—and to carry wooden canes—the symbol of chiefy authority. Nobles are expected to be laconic in their communicative interactions, speaking hardly at all in public contexts. Reserve among the Songhay is a mark of dignity and prestige: if one is a noble, following the ideal Songhay formula, he should have a spokesperson during public encounters.[2] Finally, nobles are expected to be generous to their clients, giving away their wealth even during times of scarcity.

Former slaves and foreigners, by contrast, may wear any kind of clothing. They are valued as skilled orators. Many of them are quite loquacious,

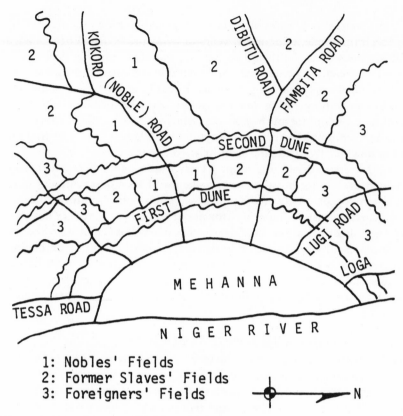

Figure 5: Distribution of fields in Mehanna

and can even be outrageous in their demands on a noble. Rather than being regarded as independent and calm, foreigners and former slaves are considered dependent and volatile.

The social exclusivity of the nobles has also played a major role in the legitimation of the chief's rule in Songhay political relations. Most Songhay believe that only someone of noble descent has the predisposition to govern. Chosen from among noble families, the Songhay chief becomes the *bankwano*. Some Songhay have likened bankwano to a cloud in which exist the sacred powers of *lakkal*, the wisdom of governance, and *fula*, the "hat" of inner strength and determination.[3] These sacred powers enable Songhay chiefs to govern effectively. When a noble is elected chief, he is said to "enter into bankwano." Once in bankwano, he is imbued with fula and lakkal, and is transformed from noble to chief; he thereby becomes the manifestation of the sacred on earth.

The focal point of Songhay politics is the chief. As the recipient of the sacred powers of *fula* and *lakkal*, which are passed down from Allah through the Prophet, the chief in Songhay has maintained power and legitimacy over the polity both by reinforcing the collective belief in his sacredness, and by demonstrating his sociopolitical effectiveness through the skillful deployment and use of clients organized in diffuse political networks.

The legitimacy of the chief, therefore, is derived from his social exclusivity and his proximity to the sacred. These important legitimating themes appear to be reified in the spatial allocation of the fields and compounds in Songhay communities. The nobles in Mehanna, for example, occupy fields along a particular road (see Figure 5). Descendants of slaves, many of whom are still clients of noble families, have their fields along those roads closest to that of the nobles. The foreigners, some of whom have become wealthy merchants, have their fields along those roads most distant from that of the nobles. The reason for this allotment of fields is purely political. Such an allotment has maintained the practice that only those Songhay with a genealogical connection to Askia Mohammed Touré— including, of course, the chief—could have fields along the noble road. Nobles, then, have fields in close proximity to the field(s) of the bankwano, who is the manifestation of the sacred on earth. Theoretically, foreigners and descendants of slaves could neither have fields along the noble road nor have compounds in the noble section of a town, which itself is situated next to the site of the Friday mosque, the most sacred space in a Songhay community. In general, the patterns found in the field allotments have been replicated, for the same political reasons, in the allotment of compounds (see Figure 6).[4]

There is, then, an inequity of access to sacred space, or to space which is at least proximate to the sacred. This inequity of access has underscored a central theme in Songhay sociopolitical relations—the basic inequality of social life, which itself highlights the social exclusivity of the nobles. Social inequality was the cement of the Songhay imperial order, and its continuation has been the foundation of the ongoing political legitimacy of Songhay nobles.[5] As the Songhay proverb states: *Boro kon go mayga windo ra, nga no mayga no* (The person who lives in [or near] the nobles' compound becomes [like a] noble). The person who has holdings close to those of the nobles—or better, close to that of the chief himself—shares in the fruits of being close to the sacred. Proximity to the space of the nobles is believed to insure divine salvation, for proximity to the sacred has always insured a person's ascension to heaven and the bounty of social effectiveness on earth.

Such continuous referencing of sociopolitical themes has made space a

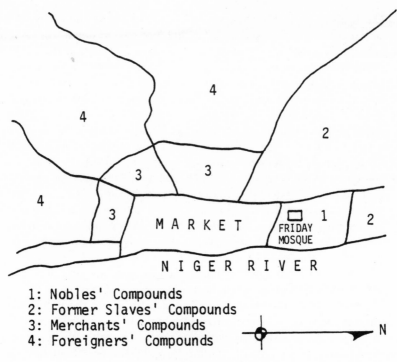

1: Nobles' Compounds
2: Former Slaves' Compounds
3: Merchants' Compounds
4: Foreigners' Compounds

Figure 6: Distribution of compounds in Mehanna

powerful political tool. Each time the descendant of slaves, for example, walks to his field, which is close to but not on the noble road, he is reminded of his social and political position in Songhay society. When he returns home, the location of his compound vis-à-vis those of nobles is a strong reminder of his social position. As this routine activity is repeated, day after day, from childhood through the various stages of the life cycle, this descendant of slaves, as Schutz would suggest, takes space for granted.[6] Space and the arrangement of objects in it becomes, for this descendant of slaves, part of the fabric of the everyday world; it becomes intertwined with his set of beliefs about the Songhay social order, a system in which social inequality is seen as part of the natural order of things. What better way for the nobles to reinforce their political legitimacy over the generations.

EXCEPTIONS AS NOISE

My initial analysis of the political use of Songhay space would lead us to believe that the Songhay nobles are firmly in control of the political system. From imperial times to the present, the nobles seem to have developed

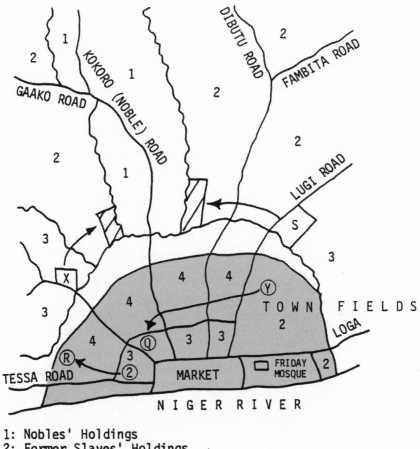

1: Nobles' Holdings
2: Former Slaves' Holdings
3: Merchants' Holdings
4: Foreigners' Holdings

Figure 7: Exceptions to the normative distribution of Songhay space

a set of symbolic media which have legitimated their authority. More specifically, I suggest that space has been one of the nobles' most powerful tools; they have used it as a medium to reinforce the collective belief that only a noble has the predisposition to govern.

Such was the gist of my initial analysis of Songhay space; it fit nicely into a more complicated web of Songhay political relations that I had been trying to explain.[7] One thorny problem remained, however. I had uncovered a number of exceptions to the normative pattern of Songhay spatial distribution (see Figure 7). Despite the fact that all the nobles had fields along one road, I discovered that merchants X and S, both of whom were of foreign origin, had taken fields next to those of the nobles. In the same vein, a former slave who was highly respected in Mehanna, Y, had moved his compound from the former slave quarter to that of the merchants. Moreover, the wealthiest merchant in Mehanna, Z, had moved his compound from the merchant neighborhood, its appropriate space, to the very outskirts of town (space R), an area designated for the poorest people of foreign origin.

Since these exceptions were so few, my immediate inclination was to treat them as though they were noise in a communication system. Noise occurs in every system of communication (and in every theory), but its presence in the communication channel in no way alters the meaning of a message being transmitted from a sender to a receiver. If I treated these exceptions as noise, I could either explain them away or ignore them, and the validity of my theory of the political use of Songhay space would be only slightly diminished.

Treating these exceptions as noise was hardly iconoclastic; this epistemological practice is evident in some of the major theoretical orientations of anthropology. French structuralists, for example, have often been criticized for the lack of importance they give to ethnographic examples which violate the fixed rules they hold to be universal. In discussing the Yanomamo Indians, Duvignaud writes:

> One is struck by the liberty demonstrated by the Indians in regard to the "elementary structures of kinship," these laws which regulate or should regulate the exchange of women between groups. They teach us that the fixed and irrepressible structures, which, according to contemporary ethnologists, regulate the members of the community, do not correspond to the complex reality of experience.[8]

In ethno-Marxism, moreover, the exception to the theory can be explained away as "fetishism," something that masks the underlying truths of the social system. For an ethno-Marxist like Godelier, "primitive" society can be reduced first to kinship relations and then, most fundamentally, to the relations of production.[9] Sahlins and Lizot, however, have demonstrated, counter to the expectations of ethno-Marxist theory, that the domestic mode of production is anti-productive; it operates below the level of its productive capacity.[10] Is this "fetishism"? The presence of these kinds of exceptions, however, has not altered the fundamental principles of structuralism or ethno-Marxism.

Treating exceptions as noise, despite the commonality of practice, turned out to be only a partial solution to the epistemological dilemma I faced. Why had I blindly accepted the notion of (Songhay) space as the reification of the social order? And was this view an accurate one?

One of the most fundamental reasons for my initial perception of Songhay space was that it has been common practice for anthropologists to see space as the static reification of the social and/or symbolic order. In his assessment of the sociocultural meaning of space, Sjoberg focused, in part, on the concrete relationships between the urban distribution of space and social organization. For Sjoberg, in the industrial city there is a direct relationship between spatial distribution and social class, the center of the city being more prestigious than the periphery. Indeed, the elite of the preindustrial city situate themselves in the central area near the governmental and religious edifices which dominate, physically and symbolically, the urban scene. As one proceeds to the outlying areas, he or she encounters members of less prestigious social classes; and on reaching the suburbs, he or she comes upon the outcasts of the preindustrial urban area.[11] Similar space-class relationships, which depict space as the reification of the social order, have been reported in studies of cities and towns in Europe, Latin America, and Africa.[12]

The anthropological literature on space also suggests a static relationship between the array of spatial patterns and beliefs about the cosmos—space as the reification of the cosmological order. Lévi-Strauss suggested that the spatial patterns found in Bororo villages reflect the dual organization of the sociosymbolic order of that society.[13] Similar assumptions are found in Griaule and Dieterlen's article on Dogon space, in which the patterns of compounds and fields are said to reify themes of Dogon cosmology.[14] In writing of African towns, Hull suggests that "community layouts mirrored the laws of nature and the forces of philosophic thought. So humane were African towns and cities that they were regarded by their inhabitants as the concrete expression of their inner thoughts about man, nature and the cosmos."[15]

Anthropologists have therefore taken a generally static approach to space and its sociocultural ramifications. In the literature, space is assumed to be "given" and "out there." While space can reify a social and/or cosmological order, it is nonetheless thought to be a relatively static, immutable phenomenon.

This anthropological orientation to space has methodological consequences. If space is "out there," then one must observe it using strictly inductive procedures. Accordingly, I conducted a door-to-door census in a number of Songhay towns, and drew an extensive map of field allotments. As I studied these data, a pattern began to emerge suggesting that the apportionment of space reified the Songhay social and symbolic order.

The source of this conceptual and methodological approach to space, I soon realized, had deeper roots than structuralism, ethno-Marxism, or functionalism. As one critically traces the history of (social) science back to its origins, he or she is struck by the ongoing influence of post-Socratic Greek philosophy. The post-Socratics, of whom Plato was the first, attempted to abstract from the flux of experience, by deductive (Plato) or inductive (Aristotle) means, a set of invariant principles which might explain observable natural phenomena.[16] This epistemological tendency, which was mirrored by my own methodological and conceptual approach to Songhay space, means that knowledge becomes idealized and removed from experience.

Given the pervasive influence of the post-Socratics, it was not surprising to discover that the static approach to the analysis of space had its source in Aristotle, who defined space as *topos*, a motionless boundary that contains an entity. To define the space of an entity, the analyst must relate it to a frame of reference—another entity or entities.[17] *Topos*, then, isolates various spatial units in a perceptual field, and the study of space is elevated to a geometric exercise.[18] Perhaps one can say that the anthropological analysis of space in society has consisted of a series of footnotes to Aristotle.

GAZING AT SONGHAY SPACE

Tempels long ago suggested that if scholars wanted to understand the nuances of "primitive" society they would have to cast aside their European (post-Socratic) visions and attempt to enter the world of the other from the other's perspective.[19] My immersion in things Songhay has convinced me that Songhay space was something other than the static reification of the social order, and that I could no longer treat exceptions to the normative distribution of space as noise in a theoretical system.

To see space from a more Songhay perspective, I adopted a more phenomenological approach. From the phenomenological vantage, the scholar "ought not to think like an external man, the psycho-physical subject who is *in* time, *in* space, or *in* society."[20] On the contrary, the scholar should attempt, through critical reflection, to transform the automatic conditioning of external stimuli into the conscious conditioning of a rational thinking subject.[21] Given critical observation, the scholar ceases to think of data only as external objects of analysis, but rather as objects the perception of which is linked dynamically to his or her own consciousness. Using this practice, scholars become aware of the biases of their socialization, and attempt to observe ethnographic happenings from the perspective of the ethnographic other. Such has been the conceptual-perceptual problem to be mastered by the Songhay ethnographer who sees roads which intersect, while his informant sees roads which end in forks.

In the phenomenological approach to spatial patterns, observers and/or social actors are no longer *in* space, but constitute it through the dynamic actions of their consciousness. For Merleau-Ponty, space is a universal force used by the constituting mind.

Space is not the setting (real or logical) in which things are arranged, but the means whereby the positing of things becomes possible. This means that instead of imagining it as a sort of ether in which all things float, or conceiving it abstractly as a characteristic they have in common, we must think of it as the universal power enabling them to be connected. . . . Is it not true that we are faced with the alternative of either perceiving things in space, or conceiving space as the indivisible system governing acts of unification performed by the constituting mind?[22]

If space is constituted by subjects living in their social worlds, what are its dynamic sociological implications? Schutz would argue that the answer lies in the relationship between space and a person's "biographically determined situation." For Schutz, a person's apprehension of space—and its sociocultural implications—would be an outgrowth of her or his "biographically determined situation" in space-time.[23] Put another way, the apprehension of space and the determination of its social meaning depend directly upon a person's potentially alterable position in the social world. Therefore, there can be, according to Schutz, "multiple realities" of space.

The "multiple realities" approach helped me to place the spatial exceptions I had uncovered into a meaningful context. If space could be a conceptual tool with important political implications for Songhay, then the people who had moved their households into inappropriate areas might well have consciously constituted space in a way different from the normative pattern—a politically competitive conception of space.

The multiple realities approach to space also allowed me to comprehend more clearly the recent activities of the merchants of foreign origin. While the social influence of the merchants had recently increased in Songhay, I had previously believed that this had had little impact on the overall politico-spatial situation. I began to reassess my initial position.

Before money was introduced as a medium of exchange in Songhay, social, economic, and political concerns were intertwined in a web of patron-client relationships. Former slaves and foreigners provided the nobles with skilled services; in return, the nobles would pay them in kind. When money was introduced into the more rural regions of Songhay just fifty years ago, merchants of foreign origin began to assert themselves in the new commercial sector, a sector which was, and continues to be, denigrated by Songhay nobles. Gradually, the merchants of foreign origin have gained control over the flow of money in Songhay and have established for themselves large networks of clients who now depend on them for their livelihood. In contemporary times, the merchants' control of money seems nearly complete, and the nobles are now in the embarrassing position of having to borrow money from the wealthier merchants in order to maintain their dwindling client networks and such symbolic requisites of office as lavish gift giving.

The overall impact of the money economy seems to have altered the "biographically determined situation" of Songhay merchants and younger descendants of slaves. Given the increasing importance of money, the merchants, with their inability to claim the sacred genealogy of the nobles, seem instead to be asserting their changing sociopolitical status by constituting space in a manner different from that of the nobles. Not all the merchants of Songhay communities are politically active, but those who are younger (ages 35 to 40 in 1981) and of foreign origin (especially Hausas who have migrated recently into Songhay from the eastern and central regions of Niger) appear to constitute space as a powerful political force. Using this concept of space, the politically active merchants, the very people responsible for the spatial exceptions, are attempting to rearrange the allotment of Songhay fields and compounds to disrupt the intricate and delicate web of themes which have in the past legitimized the rule of the Songhay nobles.

There is not, therefore, one static perception of Songhay space as the reification of the social order, but two coexisting conceptions of space, both of which have been constituted and then objectified. Songhay nobles, regardless of age or sex, continue to conceive of space as the reification of the precolonial social order. The "biographically determined situation" of the nobles *blinds* them, as theories often blind anthropologists, from *seeing* otherwise. The strategic actions of the politically active merchants to rearrange space are viewed by the nobles as ludicrous activity. In responding to a question about this phenomenon, one noble said: *Lumba tondi a si boro tey jaana* (A person cannot change a *lumba* stone into a *jaana*). While the *lumba* stone and the *jaana*, a small marine animal, are both found in the Niger River and resemble one another, there is nothing a person can do to change the stone into a living object. Just as one cannot tamper with the predetermined natural order of things, according to the noble view, one cannot alter the predestined social order of life in which only the nobles have the predisposition to govern. A similar view is held by older people who are either of foreign origin or descendants of slaves. They, too, continue to constitute space as the reification of the precolonial order of bankwano.

For foreigners and former slaves under 40 years of age in 1981, all of whom were born after the introduction of money into the Songhay economy, the actions of the politically active merchants have had a profound social impact. These younger people not only perceive the changes taking place in Songhay spatial apportionment, but are beginning themselves to participate in ongoing sociopolitical changes. In precolonial and colonial times, younger (former) slaves and foreigners would have attached themselves as clients to a noble family. Today, these younger people place themselves in the client networks of wealthy merchants. This expansion of the merchants' network of clients has enabled many of the merchants to expand their operations from the village to the regional level.

The merchant's attempt to rearrange space is part of their general challenge to the legitimacy of the Songhay nobles. Given the merchants' conception of space as a dynamic political tool, the movement of their fields and compounds to inappropriate areas is designed to transmit messages to the polity which assert (1) that space is not sacrosanct and immutable, but rather a negotiable entity; and (2) that despite the fact that they cannot share in the sacredness of bankwano, the merchants have nonetheless gained enough power to manage large networks of clients to their economic and social advantage, and to attempt to manipulate the nature of space itself.

This attempt to rearrange Songhay space also corresponds to changes in the symbolic behavior of many of the politically active merchants and former slaves. They now carry canes and often dress in white robes, as do the nobles. Their communicative behavior has become more indirect; they prefer, as do the nobles, to use intermediaries to communicate to other people or to conduct business. In short, they are using a variety of communicative media to challenge the legitimacy of the nobles.

GAZING AT ANTHROPOLOGICAL SPACE

Songhay space is constituted, rather than "given" and "out there." As a constituted conceptual force, space has been used politically by both the Songhay nobles and the politically active merchants. For the nobles, space has been constituted and objectified to reinforce the collective belief that only the nobles have the predisposition to govern. For the merchants, space has been constituted and partially objectified to challenge the political and social exclusivity of the nobles.

It could be argued that the merchants do not conceive space as a dynamic conceptual force, but rather as a static reification of the social order. Do they not want to establish a new static spatial order which is advantageous to their political interests? The point of my analysis is not to deny the very real political aspiration of the Songhay merchants, but rather to underscore the fact that they *know* how to constitute space to their political advantage. Space becomes, therefore, a force which the merchants can constitute in their attempt to reverse the social order. They have already created an alternative conception of Songhay space; and their ultimate political success may be achieved when the Songhay polity accepts the sociopolitical consequences of such an alternative conception. One cannot tamper with space if he or she perceives it passively as a static, immutable phenomenon.

My quest to see Songhay space from a more Songhay-like perspective has also been a critical examination of anthropological "seeing" which has been shaped in large measure from the postulates of post-Socratic Greek philosophy. Noncritical adoption of the methodologies and theoretical assumptions of social science can, as it did in my own case, blind the anthropologist to many of the "multiple realities" in the field situation. One solution to this pervasive epistemological problem is for anthropologists to take a more sensual perspective, allowing the visions of the other's world to penetrate their being. A more sensual gaze will not enable us to see what the ethnographic other sees, but it will produce texts that correspond more closely to the experience and perception of the ethnographic other. A critical, more sensual gaze can help us overcome the blindness that can result from post-Socratic dispositions, so that we are able to see forks as well as intersections along the road.

4 | *Signs in the Social Order: Riding a Songhay Bush Taxi*

> The lord whose oracle is at Delphi neither speaks nor conceals, but gives signs.
>
> Heraclitus

When a Western visitor to Songhay country rides a bush taxi, he or she is suddenly thrown into a social universe in which many of the advantages of being a "prestigious" European are rudely pushed aside. No matter a person's status in the pecking order of Songhay society, riding a bush taxi in Songhay is a rude initiation both to the uncomfortable conditions of public travel in the Republic of Niger and to the "hardness" of Songhay social interaction.

I took my first bush taxi ride in the fall of 1969, when I had been in the Republic of Niger a scant three weeks; I was going to depart for the town of Tera and my first teaching post. Arriving at the bush taxi depot early, I fully expected the taxi to leave on schedule. I waited impatiently for nearly thirty minutes before I asked someone in French about the hour of departure. The man to whom I had directed the question seemed to be organizing the loading operation. He smiled at me and said, "toute de suite." Reassured, I sat down under a tree and bought two oranges. One hour passed. City taxis came into the bush taxi depot and deposited more passengers bound for Tera. Young men took the baggage of these passengers and hoisted them atop the bush taxi. In my inchoate Songhay I asked the old woman sitting next to me about the hour of departure. "Who knows," she said. "In a little while." After two hours of waiting I noticed that a man, who appeared to be working on the engine of the bush taxi, was leaving the

Figure 8: A Songhay bush taxi on the Dosul to Markoy route

depot. Beside myself, I asked him where he was going. "To the autoshop. We need a new part." When I asked him when he would be back, he said, characteristically, "toute de suite." Another hour passed before the mechanic returned from the autoshop. He looked at me and said, "You should buy some meat before we get started." About 30 minutes later, another man, who had been scurrying about the depot all morning, announced that the taxi was about to depart and that all the passengers for Tera should board the taxi.

Bush taxis in the Songhay view of things are either converted Peugeot 404 pickup trucks, the carriers of which have two wooden planks secured to the floor for passenger seating, or larger vehicles called *mille kilo*, which are more like buses. Our vehicle for the ride to Tera was of the mille kilo variety. Along with the other passengers I picked up my bags and moved toward the vehicle that would transport us and our baggage to our destination. As I approached the mille kilo, three or four young boys attempted to help me with my things. When I resisted their efforts, exclaiming that I could handle my own bags, they said something to me in Songhay that I did not comprehend and then attempted to help an elderly Nigerien gentleman. He gave them his bags and gave each of them a few francs for their efforts. Inside the bus, the man who had announced our departure was telling people where they should sit. He suggested to the generous elderly gentleman that he sit next to the driver. When he saw me, he suggested that I sit next to the elderly gentleman. I said that it would be better for an old woman to sit in front of the taxi: "I'll sit in the back of the taxi like everyone else." The man looked at me strangely and told me to move on. The other passengers already seated in the back of the bus greeted me and either giggled or laughed. Meanwhile, I squeezed myself between two young mothers, both of whom were nursing their children. The noontime heat made the air hot and stuffy in the crowded mille kilo, and the baby to my left vomited on me. The driver started the engine and we began our trek to Tera, a voyage of some 190 kilometers which, because of frequent flat tires, engine breakdowns, social visits, and police stops along the way, took more than ten hours to complete.

I was too overcome by the heat, filth, and discomfort, not to mention my own ignorance of the Songhay sociocultural world, to understand what was occurring around me. As in the case of the oracle of Delphi, no one was "speaking" to me and no one was concealing anything from me; rather I found myself in an alien universe of signs, most of which I was unable to see.[1]

When I returned to Songhay in 1976 to conduct anthropological fieldwork, I continued to use public transportation. After having taken bush taxis exclusively for a two year period, I was no longer angered and irritated by long delays, engine failures, flat tires, or vomiting babies; in fact, I rather enjoyed talking with the friends I had made during all those many stops along the bush taxi route. Besides, I had gotten to know the drivers, apprentices, and personalities of the bush taxi depot. Still, I did not "read," in the sense of Ricoeur, bush taxi interaction as deeply as I might, for I was still only beginning to "see" Songhay society from a Songhay perspective.[2]

Now, almost twenty years after that first disconcerting ride, I realize that the complex interactions that form the complex of Songhay bush taxi interaction correspond to deep-seated Songhay beliefs about the nature of their social world. Much as with Geertz's Balinese cockfight or Basso's Apache jokes about white men, riding a bush taxi, a thoroughly mundane social event, can be "seen" as a set of symbolic actions that reinforce a corresponding set of Songhay cultural conceptions.[3] This chapter, like the others in this section, is not only about the dynamic mesh that connects bush taxi interaction to Songhay culture, or the mundane to the profound, but also about the epistemological process—the act of seeing—through which anthropologists and ethnographic others learn to interpret the discourse of social action.

BUSH TAXI INTERACTION IN ITS SOCIAL CONTEXT

In the twenty years since I took my first bush taxi ride in Songhay, I have learned that the identities involved in any bush taxi interaction are all tied in one way or another to the history of the Songhay Empire. Some of the passengers in a mille kilo headed toward Tera, for example, are bound to be of noble blood. The taxi drivers, the apprentice drivers, and the taxi loaders, by contrast, are likely to be either descendants of former slaves or foreigners (*yeowey*).

In many ways the past intersects with the present when the members of these separate, but putatively unequal, social groups interact in any number of mundane social events including, of course, riding a bush taxi. In the previous chapter, I described how one's social grouping affects his or her apprehension of space. Here I would like to focus on how one's social grouping affects his or her social behavior. Nobles are supposed to be reserved, laconic, and generous. Former slaves and foreigners are expected to be outgoing, loquacious, and stingy. These culturally denoted expectations of ideal noble/non-noble interaction have a major bearing on the kind of social activities the son of Askia, as compared to a son of a (former) slave, might engage in. To this day most nobles do not deign to engage in commercial activities; they would rather be represented by an intermediary.[4] Former slaves and foreigners have participated fully in the money economy, which was introduced into the rural areas of Songhay some fifty years ago and today forms the foundation of the local economy. The noble, therefore, might well be a passenger on a bush taxi, but former slaves and foreigners are almost always the drivers, loaders, or owners of transport vehicles.

The foregoing description suggests that the structure of Songhay is relatively static, the ideal behavioral expectations of the noble and non-nobles having produced and maintained unequal and exclusive social categories. The close "reading-seeing" of the symbolic interactions below, however, suggests that, in Songhay social interaction within non-noble groups, notions of status and role are not rigidly fixed by ideal cultural categories and behavioral expectations.

LOADING BUSH TAXIS IN BONFEBBA

Men load cargo and people in bush taxis every Friday in the village of Bonfebba, which is situated on the east bank of the Niger River in Songhay. On Friday, which is market day, traders and travelers from the west bank, known in Songhay as *haro banda* (behind the water), come to Bonfebba by dugout to participate in market activities or to travel by bush taxi to such urban centers as Tillaberi and Niamey, which are located to the south.[5] While the cast of characters who load bush taxis may change from week to week, the mechanics of bush taxi loading remain fairly constant. A bush taxi cannot be loaded, obviously, if there are no passengers or cargo. But if there is cargo and if passengers do appear, then they must come in contact with people associated with bush taxis at market towns. There is the *coxeur*, who collects money from the passengers and who directs the actual loading of the taxi. The coxeur typically has one or two assistants who place the small cargo into the taxi and tie the more bulky cargo onto the taxi's roof. The assistants to the coxeur often hire their own assistants. The passenger, therefore, often comes in contact with the coxeur's assistants' assistants. Each taxi, of course, has a driver, someone who has obtained his driver's permit and who knows very well how to repair automobile engines. The driver always has his personal assistant, who is called the *apprenti*. To become a driver one must serve a several-year apprenticeship.

All of the actors in the bush taxi drama maintain some notion about the status and expectations of their social role. But as the following description indicates, the notion of status and the expectations it carries is negotiable.

SOGA (COXEUR):	Hey everybody, hey! Come here. Tillaberi people. Niamey people. Come here quickly. We must go. We will not wait.

((Passenger A presents herself to Soga))

SOGA:	Where are you going, woman?
PASSENGER A:	I'm going to Tillaberi.

SOGA: Hand over the money, 600 francs.

PASSENGER A: ((laughs)) There is not enough [money]. Lower your
                         price.

SOGA: ((looking around)) Zakarey? Where is he? ((sees Zaka-
                         rey, his assistant)) Come here!

((Zakarey arrives at the taxi))

SOGA: Zakarey, put the bags on top [of the bush taxi].

ZAKAREY: Okay.

SOGA: ((talking to the woman, Passenger A)) Go over there to
                         wait, woman.

*((Soga goes into the market to look for passengers. Passengers B, C, and D
present themselves))*

SOGA: Where are you going

PASSENGER B: Niamey.

PASSENGER C: Tillaberi.

PASSENGER D: Karma.

SOGA: The one going to Karma, 750 francs. The one going to
                         Tilla, 600 francs. The one going to Niamey, 950 francs

*((The passengers give Soga the money without an argument; they know the
standard prices.))*

SOGA: Zakarey. Go and fetch Boreyma. We need two people
                         to carry the passengers' things.

*((All the passengers, nine in total, are waiting around the bush taxi while
Zakarey and Boreyma, another assistant, hoist goods and personal baggage up
to the roof of the taxi. The driver is nowhere in sight.))*

PASSENGER C: When are we going to go? It is necessary that I arrive
                         in Niamey before noon.

SOGA: Patience man. Patience. ((looking around the market))
                         Okay. Everyone get in the bush taxi. . . . Boreyma,
                         show the people where they should sit.

((Soga inspects the seating arrangement.))

SOGA: It is not good. Alfa Adoulaye! You must not sit in the
                         back. Come here. Sit in the cabin [i.e., next to the
                         driver in the most comfortable seat].

PASSENGER D: Where is the driver? We must go.

SOGA: Patience ((looks for the driver)). Good, he is coming
                         now.

*((The driver arrives and greets Soga, Zakarey, Boreyma, and a few of the
passengers. He opens the hood of the bush taxi and looks under the vehicle to
inspect the suspension and the tires.))*

SOGA: Has everyone paid?

((Soga looks into the taxi and counts the money he has collected.))

DRIVER: Okay, Soga. How much [money] do you have?
SOGA: There is 6500 francs.
DRIVER: In God's name, it is not enough, Soga.
SOGA: It is enough!
((The driver gets into the taxi. Soga explains to him where each person is going and how much each has paid.))
BOREYMA: ((pointing to a man in the back of the taxi)) Soga, you forgot that man.
SOGA: ((in a loud voice)) I did not forget anyone. You [Boryema] are a donkey. . . . ((looking at the driver)) Is it good?
((The driver goes through the money, takes out 500 francs in 100-franc coins, and gives them to Soga.))
SOGA: ((screaming)) It will not do! There is not enough money. You give some more.
DRIVER: ((smiles at Soga)) The owner does not agree, you know.
((The driver closes the window of the taxi. While Soga and Boreyma try to force open the window, the driver starts the engine and drives away.))
SOGA: That man [the driver] is not easy [i.e., is hard]. He is not good.
ZAKAREY: Where's my cut?
BOREYMA: And mine?
((Boreyma grabs Soga while Zakarey searches his pockets.))
BOREYMA: It is the money we want. Hand it over.
SOGA: ((gives them each 100 francs)) You get 100 francs.
BOREYMA: It is not enough! It is not enough!
ZAKAREY: Soga, you, too, are a donkey. You must increase [our cut].
SOGA: ((smiles at Zakarey and Boreyma)) If you are not agreed [to the amount], go and look for work again [i.e., somewhere else].[6]

In this interaction, Soga, the coxeur, is the focal point. By following closely what Soga does and says, one can uncover interactional patterns not uncommon in everyday Songhay life. To begin with, neither the owner nor the driver, the two most highly ranked social identities in the transport pecking order, is present for the entire episode. During most of the interaction, therefore, Soga the coxeur is in authority. Throughout the loading, Soga attempts to maintain his social prestige as coxeur, as reflected in his use of language that is laced with requests and demands.

Since Soga knows the owner's prices, he will neither bargain with the woman, which would reveal his symbolic weakness, nor load the baggage onto the roof of the taxi, which would be a symbolic reflection of inferior status. For the physical labor involved in loading the taxi, Soga hired, on his own initiative, two assistants. Soga's language to his two assistants—his requests and his demands—suggests that he perceives that he is in authority and is maintaining his social prestige.

Soga's authority is diminished greatly, however, when the driver returns to the taxi. As soon as the driver arrives Soga makes his first request for information other than the destination of the passengers, asking if everyone has paid. The driver ignores this and asks the coxeur how much money he has collected. When Soga tells him the amount, the driver replies that the coxeur is short. Here the implication is that either Soga might have pocketed the money, a veiled insult, or the driver, knowing that 6500 francs is the correct amount, is trying to shame the coxeur while asserting his own prestige as driver. Boreyma, sensing the driver's motive, tries to take advantage of the situation by asserting that Soga has forgotten to collect money from one passenger, a rather direct challenge to Soga's competence and authority. Soga, reacting to Boreyma's assertion and wishing to maintain face, insults his assistant, calling him a donkey; he then asserts that he has forgotten no one. The driver accepts this and gives Soga 500 francs for his work. Soga is angry with the driver for paying a coxeur so little money—an insult to his competence and skill as coxeur. But the driver absolves himself; the owner, the ultimate, albeit absent, authority, is the person who sets the prices for passage, for cargo, and for coxeurs. Despite the near-violent protests of Soga and his assistants, the driver leaves Bonfebba, having used this brief scene to reinforce his authority—at the expense of Soga.

The give and take of Songhay bush taxi loading is not yet complete, however. Soga's assistants want their money. They begin to play the kind of game Soga played only a minute earlier with the driver. Soga, once again in authority, must be firm. He gives each assistant 100 francs, and suggests that if they are not happy with this amount they should search elsewhere for work. Here, Soga uses the strong, full tone of assertions and demands rather than the pleading questions of angry but powerless assertions.

Beneath the surface of the episode, however, appears an ethos of "hardness," examples of which are expressed throughout the scene. Soga speaks harshly to the woman who cannot pay the required price for the trip to Tillaberi; he tells her to go and sit under a tree, and no one comes to her aid. The taxi driver expresses little sympathy toward Soga by giving the coxeur an unsuitable fee for his services; indeed, he expresses his contempt for Soga and his assistants by rapidly shutting his taxi window, literally closing himself off from his social inferiors. Soga also treats his assistants crudely, barking orders at them as though they were donkeys. Soga's assistants attempt to insult him in public. The result of all of this "hardness" is that people are either shaming others or being shamed in public contexts. From brief exposure to this typical slice of Songhay bush taxi loading, we confront a Songhay social arena—the marketplace—that is not only "hard," but crude and harsh as well.[7]

DEEP AND SURFACE READINGS OF BUSH TAXI INTERACTION

To uncover the deep meanings of bush taxi loading, we must understand how elements of interaction express meanings at various levels of cultural significance. Readers of bush taxi interaction must therefore attempt to understand "not another person, but a project, that is, the outline of new being-in-the-world."[8] Put another way, the deep readers of Songhay bush taxi interaction must come to understand what people are "saying" to one another and how this "saying" corresponds to those signs that make the world comprehensible.[9] To approach a more profound "reading" of bush taxi loading, we must journey beyond the analysis of surface discourse and attempt to "see" how this discourse, in the words of Bachelard, "reverberates" in the pit of Songhay being.[10] If we wish to "seize the reality of an image" to see how it "reverberates" in the pit of (Songhay) being, we must consider the metaphorical aspects of symbolic expression.[11]

The analysis of metaphor is "perhaps the most perplexing, vexed and intractable question in the whole philosophy of language."[12] Despite the embryonic state of metaphorical theory, we can say that metaphors are tropes that, by linking two seemingly unrelated semantic domains, forge a new meaning.[13] Further, the metaphor may also juxtapose "elements of a concrete image in order to formulate some set of more abstract relationships."[14] Metaphor appears to be a central cognitive mechanism that can provide the organizing images that render experience intelligible.[15] It is for this reason that elements of metaphor can be found in ordinary discourse: "Metaphor permeates all discourse, ordinary and special, and we should have a hard time finding a purely literal paragraph anywhere."[16] Johnson and Lakoff suggest, moreover, that metaphors "structure what we perceive, how we get around, and how we relate to one another."[17] Metaphors therefore seem to structure the relationships among many of the objects, concepts, and/or social others we confront in our experience.

Bush Taxis, Metaphors, and Songhay Proverbs

It is clear that people do not speak entirely in metaphors. In the sentence, "the chairman plowed through the meeting," the word "plowed" is the only unequivocally metaphorical element in an otherwise literal sentence.[18] In the bush taxi event, it is equally clear that the interactants are not speaking primarily in metaphors. If we reread the sequences presented above, however, we can isolate a number of relationships structured through metaphors. If we then juxtapose those relationships to a number of corresponding Songhay proverbs and idiomatic expressions, we can see more deeply into the interaction.

Consider, first of all, the relationship between TIME and PATIENCE, which finds expression in the following items from the interaction as well as from a number of Songhay proverbs and idioms.

Example 1.   Q: When are you leaving?
              A: Patience, patience.

Example 2.   Q: When is the driver coming?
              A: In a little while. Have patience.

Example 3.   Old men have patience.

Example 4.   Men without patience die young.

Example 5.   Youth are always in a hurry; they have no patience.

These statements consider time on two levels. Time is considered in a chronemic manner, as in examples 1, and 2, in which the request for information as to when X is coming or when X is going is answered not by a distinct time (noon, 3:30) but by the exhortation, "patience." This answer reflects the more fundamental relationship in Songhay thought between time-in-life and patience. "Old men have patience," hence they understand the meaning of time, for "men without patience die young" and "youth are always in a hurry" (i.e., they lack patience). The metaphorically structured statements about time that I have isolated, however, seem not to refer—even tangentially—to Songhay beliefs about time and wisdom, age and wisdom, or the sweep of time from the mythic origins of Songhay to the present. Beliefs about time and wisdom and age and wisdom seem to be more connected to the metaphoric elements found in proverbs. Notions of Songhay mythic time are even further removed from surface discourse; they are embodied in the symbolic movement of such ritual as possession dance, magic rites, and circumcision. Symbolic "motion thus becomes a metaphor, one's time being enacted within another, distilling myth, incarnating it in the process of being enacted."[19] The surface discourse of the bush taxi interaction, therefore, presents us with an opening to deeper levels of metaphoric interpretation.

The second metaphoric relationship that I have isolated in the loading sequence concerns MEN and DONKEYS. In the slice of interaction presented above, Soga says to Boreyma:

Example 6.   You [Boreyma] are a donkey

Later in the interaction, Boreyma returns the compliment. There are other statements in Songhay speech in which human activities are understood (unfavorably) in terms of those of donkeys:

Example 7.   Your head and a donkey's head; it is the same thing.

Example 8.   You are the son of a donkey.

From these examples, which can serve as real or ritual insults, we understand that the activities of human beings who are slow-witted are seen in light of the behavior of donkeys.[20] But the observation of human beings interacting with donkeys and a perusal of Songhay proverbs sheds more light, it seems, on the relationship of MEN and DONKEYS. Donkeys have no dignity in the natural order. Many Songhay throw stones at donkeys, and sometimes beat them on the head with *batons* for no apparent reason. Donkeys are abused and are expected to work incessantly, as is suggested by the following proverb.

Example 9.   Even while the donkey is resting, there is a load on its back.

By juxtaposing a number of relevant Songhay proverbs with the analysis of the symbolic expression found in the bush taxi episode, we flesh out the relationship of men to donkeys. In everyday language, Songhay are not likely to use sentences that highlight the similarity of the behavior of some men to that of donkeys.

The third metaphoric relationship I have isolated concerns MEN and ROCKS. In everyday language, and in the bush taxi interaction, men and their behavior can be conceived in terms of a rock, that which is hard, not easy to move, or intractable.

Example 10.   The man is not easy [is hard].[21]

Example 11.   His hands are hard.

Example 12.   He has inner strength [fula]; he is not easy.

To be hard is a desirable quality in Songhay social life: one is respected if he or she is tough, resolute, and successful in asserting his/her will, just as the taxi driver asserts his will in his interaction with Soga. Despite his "hardness," however, the driver does not want to be held responsible for the low wages he gives to Soga and his assistants. He therefore tells them that the owner is the one who sets the prices; someone external to the immediate context, the driver is "saying," is responsible for your grief and misfortune. A hard man is capable of mercy if mercy does not jeopardize his social position. The ethos of "hardness" is therefore not limited to market discourse; it is anchored to an important conception of Songhay social life, a conception that, at its foundation, is metaphorically structured.

NONLINGUISTIC METAPHORS AND SONGHAY SYMBOLIC INTERACTION

Metaphors, Songhay and otherwise, can be nonlinguistic as well as linguistic.[22] The examination of the language used in the Bonfebba bush taxi loading does provide us with some significant insights. We do get the connection of time and patience, men and donkeys, and men and rocks. The more substantive statements of these metaphoric relationships are brought forth in proverbs (example 9) and idiomatic expressions (examples 3, 4, 5, 12) that were not directly expressed during the bush taxi loading.

Proceeding deeper, we arrive at the threshold of metaphorically structured symbolic interaction. Here, the comportment of the interactant is considered as a whole. We already know that the relationship of men to rocks ("hardness") is metaphorically structured. What about the notion of money and hardness? If we relied on strictly linguistic information, we would not isolate a relationship between money and "hardness"; but if we consider the total scope of symbolic expression, the relationship between money and "hardness" stares us in the face. Soga, for example, is "hard" in his interaction with the passengers. He uses short, curt sentences with them and will not negotiate prices. The driver acts "hard" when he deals with Soga. In both cases, "hardness" as a set of behaviors is associated with money and its handling.

Probing still deeper into the Songhay world of meaning, we see that "hardness" and social negotiation are interconnected. There are a number of instances in which Soga's assistants attempt to exceed the limits of their social role. Boreyma does just this when he suggests that Soga, a professional *coxeur*, has forgotten to collect money from one man. Soga realizes this affront and puts Boreyma in his place by calling him a donkey.

In general, this kind of social negotiation and attempt at status manipulation is highly characteristic of the Songhay marketplace; it pervades the loading of a bush taxi. Passengers, for example, must be seated in symbolic patterns. If the appropriate pattern is violated, as when an Islamic cleric had been seated in the rear of the taxi, clearly a position designated for someone of a lesser social status, the situation must be corrected in a "hard" way. The driver's interaction with Soga, moreover, is a clear case of social negotiation—the driver inflates his public status at the expense of Soga, who before the arrival of the driver had been "hard" and in control.

Despite the aura of social negotiation, the people associated with loading a bush taxi go only so far. While Boreyma, Soga, and the driver manipulate Songhay symbolic expression to gain as much monetary prestige as possible, when all is literally said and done, no one has progressed. The driver still maintains his superior status vis-à-vis Soga, who remains in a position superior to that of Boreyma and Zakarey. The absentee owner controls the entire group; he sets the prices and the payment schedules. Correspondingly, the social interaction of bush taxi loading exhibits negotiation, but the rights and duties of many of the roles remain by and large fixed—controlled by external forces. This extremely important conception of Songhay everyday reality concerning the immobility of the social order is not referenced in everyday language, but through the deep "reading" of experience day in and day out.

Foreigners and former slaves cannot become nobles; coxeurs do not become drivers. There are, of course, exceptions to this pattern in the commercial sector: some assistants do become coxeurs; apprentices become drivers; some drivers become owners. But these upward transitions are rare, in the Songhay view of things, and the odds are in favor of role stagnation rather than role transformation. The notion of immobility corresponds to the Songhay notion that life in general is controlled by forces outside the self. One's putative progress in life in the commercial sector depends on the whims of another (in the case of Soga, on the whims of the driver and the absentee owner). Immobility, therefore, is a central concept of the relations of self to the Songhay social world.

With the notion of immobility, we are again confronted with a static representation of the Songhay social order. If the Songhay's fate is ascribed at his or her birth, then his or her social category is fixed. This static representation of the Songhay social order seems inaccurate, however. As we have seen, Songhay actors publicly manipulate symbolic expression to inflate their public status, however fleetingly, at the expense of the social other. Perhaps it would be more fitting to say that Songhay immobility seems to represent a set of invariable brackets within which social negotiation takes place. Former slaves cannot become nobles, but if they are crafty negotiators in the commercial sector, they can become noblelike.[23]

Moving another step deeper into the Songhay scheme of things, we can appreciate more fully the connection of social negotiation to hardness. In the past nobles were "hard" warriors (*wangari*); today their comportment is a demonstration of the noble attribute *fula*, inner strength and intractability. Similarly, former slaves and foreigners demonstrate the "hardness" of Songhay social interaction, challenging one another if only for a brief moment of social prestige, as in Boreyma's challenge to Soga. Generally speaking, the "harder" a person is, the more prestige he or she gathers; and the more prestige he or she gathers, the more noblelike he or she becomes. These, then, are the cross currents in Songhay society. The social order is arranged in ascribed and generally exclusive social categories of unequal rank; the nobles are exclusive of the foreigners and the former slaves; and human interaction in this ascribed social order is characterized by a high degree of social negotiation. Former slaves will sometimes challenge the "face" of the nobles, and they sometimes win a momentary victory.[24] The former slave's victorious encounter with a son of Askia is illusory, however, for when all is said and done, not much has changed. The former slave can never claim to have the blood of the Askias running in his veins.

READING AND METAPHORIC LINKAGES

"Reading," in the sense I am using here, is an aspect of the kind of critical observation that I am advocating in this book. In my own case my first "reading" of Songhay bush taxi interaction had little to do with the Songhay and more to do with my own set of admittedly ethnocentric predispositions. Anthropologists, for the most part, are keenly aware of their cultural blindness when they are first exposed to another culture. The accumulation of knowledge through fieldwork enables most of us to focus our vision of the other culture. But fieldwork experiences, however exceptional they might be, do not guarantee a deep comprehension of another culture. Deeper "readings" of bush taxi interaction, for example, must correspond to deeper experiences in the Songhay world, for "we must say that the meaningful patterns which a depth-interpretation wants to grasp cannot be understood without a kind of personal commitment similar to that of the reader who grasps the depth semantics of a text and makes it is own."[25] This commitment, it seems to me, is not to use what one can discover about the Songhay or any other group to prove or disprove a universal truth, but to take a sensual turn, letting the other's world penetrate us.

Such a commitment is more than the anthropologist's attempt to master the other's language. As any sociolinguist would suggest, there is more to learning a language than studying its phonology and grammar. To be able to use a language, one must immerse oneself in both *langue* and *parole* and learn both linguistic and sociolinguistic rules.[26] Going one step further, one could say that for deep "readers" to make the text their own, they must begin to grasp the metaphoric linkages, the "reverberations" that are expressed in discourse.

It is perhaps the emergence of expressivity that constitutes the marvel of language. . . . There is no mystery in language. The most poetic, most "sacred" language operates with the same semic variables as the most banal word of the dictionary. But there is a mystery of language. It is that language says, says something, says something of being. If there is an enigma of symbolism it resides entirely at the level of manifestation where the equivocity of being becomes said in discourse.[27]

The more I have learned about Songhay language, the better I have become able to place the symbolic interactions of such mundane activities as loading a bush taxi into deeper perspectives. This vantage has revealed to me the full significance of "hardness" and its relation to social negotiation. Perhaps the importance of a sensual approach to anthropological inquiry is that as a process it continually reveals to the anthropologist the limitations of his or her knowledge. After more than forty-five years of commitment to the Songhay world, Jean Rouch is still trying to solve many of the mysteries of the Songhay cosmos. Such commitment is probably beyond the expectations and hopes of most American anthropologists who must compete for dwindling research funds. But without this commitment to "language," or to "deep visions," which may take years to develop, how can we be sure that what we claim to know is indeed knowledge? As one of my Songhay teachers once told me: "If you listen to us, you will learn much about our ways. But to have vision, you must grow old with us." As the discipline of anthropology proceeds from crisis to crisis, it might be beneficial to remember the aphorism of Heraclitus and confront fully those signs we encounter daily in the field.

5 Son of Rouch: Songhay Visions of the Other

Imagine an anthropological discourse in which the others classify their anthropologists in the same way that we classify them. Such a movement would be a step toward the decolonization of anthropological texts; it would also help infuse our writing with a desperately needed sense of humor. "Savages," after all, enjoy savaging their ethnographers.

In earlier pages I have written about how the Eurocentric gaze affected the perception and analysis of my Songhay field experiences. In this chapter I argue that "their" classifications of "us" are revelatory, for they situate ethnographic research in a broader, more epistemologically and politically sensitive context. I explore here what it meant for the Songhay to label me the "son" of French filmmaker and anthropologist Jean Rouch.

IMAGES OF JEAN ROUCH

In 1941, when he was a young engineer working for the French Travaux Publics in the colony of Niger, Jean Rouch had his first contact with the Songhay people in the Niamey Region of Niger. With the aid of his mentors, Marcel Griaule and Théodore Monod, and his informant-friends, especially Damoré Zika, Rouch gathered information on Songhay mythology and language. By 1942 he had amassed a collection of documentary photographs and ritual objects used in Songhay possession ceremonies. After the war, Rouch returned to Songhay country, and in 1946–47 Jean Sauvy, Pierre Ponty, and Rouch took a dugout the entire length of the Niger River. Back in Songhay in 1948, he toured the Tillaberi region, visiting the most important districts. In Sangara and Wanzerbé he met the famous sorcerers of Songhay, the sohanci, the direct patrilineal descendants of the great

Figure 9: "Son of Rouch" in Niamey, Niger, 1976 (photo by Cheryl Olkes)

Songhay king, Sonni Ali Ber. Rouch also conducted fieldwork among the Songhay in 1949 when he went to Aribinda and Dori (Burkina Faso) and Hombori (Mali). This trip enabled him to complete his work on Songhay mythology. In 1950–51, he studied the Songhay populations living in what was then the Gold Coast, and he continued this work in 1953–55.

This early work resulted in an ethnographic treasure chest of materials. Rouch published two studies, *Contribution à l'histoire des Songhay* (1953), which focused upon Songhay archeology, mythology, and history, and *Les Songhay* (1953), a classic ethnography. In 1960 he published his *thèse d'état*, *La Religion et la magie Songhay*, the culmination of almost twenty years of contact with Songhay. *La Religion* is a comprehensive ethnography, covering in exhaustive detail Songhay mythology, possession, and sorcery. *La Religion* is a book alive with the voices of Rouch's 67 informants, whose words are woven throughout the text; Rouch's own voice is subdued. His interpretations are limited to a short preface and an even shorter conclusion.

This Griaulian predisposition to let the informant speak, to let the informant evoke his/her world, paved the way for Rouch's contributions to a more evocative medium: ethnographic film. The early years produced some of Rouch's most memorable films: *Initiation à la danse des possédés*

(1948), *Circoncision* (1949), *Bataille sur le grand fleuve* (1953), *Les Hommes qui font la pluie* (1951), and *Les Magiciens de Wanzerbé* (1949). *Les Magiciens de Wanzerbé* has a remarkable sequence of a sorcerer's dance (*sohanci hori*) in which a dancer vomits his magical chain and then swallows it. Like Rouch's other films, *Les Magiciens* documents the horrors and delights of the Songhay worlds of sorcery and possession, worlds in which the inexplicable occurs with alarming frequency.[1]

With the exception of a few articles, Rouch has, since 1960, concentrated exclusively on ethnographic filmmaking.[2] Fieldwork in Ghana and the Ivory Coast resulted in three incomparable films: *Les Maîtres fous* (1954), *Jaguar* (1954), and *Moi, Un Noir* (1954). Fieldwork in Niger between 1957 and 1964 culminated in his well-known *Chasse au lion à l'arc* (The Lion Hunters). Rouch has also produced feature-length general audience films based partially upon his ethnographic experience (see *Petit à petit* [1968] and *Cocorico, monsieur poulet* [1974]), which were commercial successes in France and in West Africa. Most of Rouch's film work is concentrated on Songhay possession, Rouch's ethnographic passion. There are cinematic interviews with possession priests (*Douda Sorko*), and a score of short films on the Songhay *yenaandi* ceremonies, the possession rites during which the spirits are asked to bring rain.

Among the most fascinating of Rouch's films is *Tourou et bitti* (1971). The film covers the closing moments of the fourth day of a festival for the *genji bi* (the black spirits, which control soil fertility and pestilence). During the first three days, the spirits refused to possess their mediums, a bad sign for the upcoming harvest. Sido, the Simiri possession priest, invited Rouch to attend the rites on the fourth day of the festivities. Nothing happened until just before sunset, when Rouch began to film. Suddenly, as if in response to the presence of the camera, one of the black spirits took the body of his medium. Rouch says he himself entered a "cine-trance," which facilitated possession.[3] Aside from making important points about the phenomenology of the self, this film also documented Jean Rouch's power in Songhay.

In Europe Rouch's books, his articles and especially his films have brought him international acclaim. He is considered the creator of *cinéma verité*, and if he is not the greatest ethnographic filmmaker today—and I think that he is—he is certainly the most prolific, with more than 100 films to his credit. In Niger he has become a legend, his name evoking both positive and negative passions. Many Nigeriens are proud of the powerful images that Jean Rouch's films depict; others, who are profoundly insulted, complain that his films reinforce the "primitive" imagery of African peoples. His films have nonetheless been shown in all the regions of Niger. Jean Rouch has introduced both Nigerien and European audiences to the fascinating peoples of Niger.

While Europeans applaud Jean Rouch as an artistic innovator, Songhay consider him in an altogether different light. He is, to quote one of my teachers in Wanzerbé, "the European who follows the spirits." For many Songhay, Rouch is the shrewd European who had the foresight to take seriously the Songhay world of power. "It is not mere coincidence," a spirit possession priest told me in Tillaberi, "that Rouch is a big man [*boro beri*]; he has power. The spirits clear for him his path."

In his writings Rouch admits that his deep penetration into the Songhay world, his access to worlds of unimaginable power devolves from the spirits.

> But, when the moment comes that the observer becomes a simple spectator among other spectators, when the moment comes when he speaks and understands the language sufficiently to know what is being said and to respond to it sometimes, he *participates* just like his neighbors. And so it follows that at each possession dance that I witnessed, the deities came to greet me as well as my neighbors and spoke at length to me.[4] (my emphasis)

Rouch also comments on his entry into the Songhay world of sorcery:

> The penetration of more circumspect domains, like the magician's milieu, posed other problems. After a slow and gradual approach, contact could be established (with the aid of the intervention of the deities in the course of a possession dance). Slowly, I entered the game, but as soon as certain doors opened before me, they would close behind me, prohibiting all retreats and cutting all ties with the outside. The observer was completely overwhelmed by what he observed. Was this still a matter of observation?[5]

Rouch's penetration of a world of great power in Wanzerbé was an event that commanded attention. Word spread widely in Songhay: Rouch had been to Wanzerbé. Rouch had learned great secrets. Rouch had eaten kusu, the substance of power. Rouch was a man to be both feared and respected. Over time many Songhay have blended the notion of "Rouch" into the imagery of myth; he has become part of contemporary Songhay cosmology. When I returned from my initial visit to Wanzerbé, thirty years after Jean Rouch's first visit there, the news spread widely in Songhay: Stoller had been to Wanzerbé. Stoller had learned great secrets. Stoller had eaten kusu. Stoller was a man to be both feared and respected. Stoller had become the "son of Rouch."

ROUCH AND HIS "SON"

I suppose I was destined to meet Jean Rouch sooner or later. It happened for the first time in August of 1976, when I went to Niger for my doctoral study with the Songhay. Having read his books and seen some of his films, I felt honored to make his acquaintance. He immediately put me at ease and encouraged me, saying that my research project was an important one.

So I prepared to begin my fieldwork in Mehanna, a riverine village some 180 kilometers north of Niamey. My arrival there sparked a discussion about my lodgings.

"You could live in the *campement*," Tondi Bello, the village chief told me.

"Yes," said his crony Saadu, "that's where Monsieur Rouch stayed when he came to Mehanna."

"Monsieur Rouch?" I wondered aloud.

"Yes." replied Tondi Bello. "Until you came Monsieur Rouch was the only European to spend time here."

"When was that?"

"Oh, that was thirty years ago."

"Thirty years ago. I see."

"Do you want to stay at the *campement?*" Saadu asked.

"He doesn't want to stay there," interjected Boreyma Boulhassane, who had shared the cabin of the truck that had transported me to Mehanna that morning. "He should stay in my family's compound; it's in the center of town."

"But Monsieur Rouch stayed in the *campement*," Saadu complained.

"Monsieur Paul, where do you want to stay?"

"In town." I realized at that point that I needed to try to follow an independent path.

My work proceeded smoothly, although it was disquieting when people categorized my efforts in terms of Monsieur Rouch. When I began working with Zeinabou Djiketa, the possession troupe priestess in Mehanna, she immediately told me that Monsieur Rouch had visited her compound thirty years before.

"Yes, Monsieur Rouch came here when my mother was the priestess. He asked us to take out all our possession objects [hatchets with bells, costumes, sabers, antelope horns]. We took them out, and he took photographs of them. He paid us some money and we gave him a few of our objects."

Seizing this opportunity, I asked her if I could do what Monsieur Rouch had done nearly thirty years before. She refused, claiming that the possession objects had deteriorated; they were not fit to be photographed.

In March of 1977 I decided to visit the fabled village of Wanzerbé, the center of unequaled Songhay sorcery. (A trip to Wanzerbé in 1979 is described in Chapter 2.) Unbridled romantic that I was, I decided to travel to Wanzerbé on horseback, a 120-kilometer trip. My guide was Idrissa Dembo, who was born in Wanzerbé. Idrissa was a felicitous choice as my guide, for his stepmother is the illustrious Kassey, the most powerful sorcerer in Wanzerbé. My working with Kassey would be a real ethnographic coup,

since for thirty years she had stedfastly refused to work with researchers—
Rouch, other Europeans, and Nigeriens alike. We spent two hot and dusty
days in the saddle and finally arrived in the compound of Idrissa Dembo's
father. We were greeted warmly and fed well. In the evening, men from the
neighborhood came by to visit.

"You came here on horseback?" one asked.

"Yes."

"Monsieur Rouch used to come here on horseback. Do you know him?"

"I've met him," I responded.

"He used to ride in from Ayoru. Where did you come from?"

"Mehanna."

"Why didn't you come from Ayoru, like Monsieur Rouch? Mehanna is
too far."

"Yes, it is," I responded.

"Are you going to do what Monsieur Rouch did?"

"Not exactly."

Another man joined our discussion. He greeted me and then asked. "Do
you know Monsieur Rouch?"

"Yes."

"Where is he?"

"I don't know."

"We haven't seen him in a long time."

"How long?"

"Many years. Say hello to him from us here in Wanzerbé, will you?"

"I'll be sure to do it," I told him.

The morning after my arrival I learned that Kassey had left town that
morning, and would not return until after my departure. A wasted trip!
Idrissa suggested that we visit the hunters at Youmboum, a permanent
water hole just to the north of the village of Yatakala. We mounted our
horses and rode to Youmboum. There, I was introduced to Monsieur
Rouch's *godji* (monochord violinist) Issiakia, and his brother Wangari, two
of the protagonists in Rouch's monumental *Chasse au lion à l'arc* (1957–65).
Issiakia took me to an abandoned mudbrick house at the north end of the
lake.

"This is where Monsieur Rouch stayed," he told me. We went inside
and I saw some electric wire attached to the closed window shutter.

"What's that?" I asked.

"Monsieur Rouch put it there. He had a machine that made light."

"I see."

"Do you know Monsieur Rouch?" Issiakia asked.

"Yes, I do."

"Do you know when he's coming back?"

"No, I don't."

We returned to Issiakia's house. "When Monsieur Rouch was here, I always played my violin for him. My brother, Wangari, sang praise-songs. Shall we play for you?"

I took out my tape recorder, and Issiakia played his violin. Wangari sang about the hunter's poison and the great hunters of the past. This musical poetry was familiar to me; I had seen the same performance in a Jean Rouch film.

We returned to Wanzerbé, whereupon we came across the grandson of Mossi Bana, the sohanci who had been Rouch's principal informant in the village of sorcerers.

"Are you French?" he asked me, never having seen me before.

"No, I'm American."

"Well, we don't want any more films. We are tired of your damn films. And if you want to talk with my father [Halidu Bana], you will have to pay at least 50,000 francs CFA."

This man was one of the people who felt that Rouch's films did not portray Wanzerbé in a favorable light. (Six years later Kassey told me: "We don't like films. We don't want strangers laughing at us.")

"I did not come here to make films," I told him. "I came to meet the people here. That's all. I'm not a filmmaker, and I don't take people's pictures unless they agree to it. I am not Monsieur Rouch, damn it!"

"We don't want your films," he persisted.

For Mossi Bana's grandson, the myth of Rouch was insurmountable. I left Wanzerbé completely frazzled.[6]

In 1979 I had a talk with Issaka Boulhassane, an elder living in Mehanna. A noble, Issaka Boulhassane has matrilineal ties to people from Wanzerbé. The famous Kassey is his maternal aunt. I described my work to him. He complimented me on my command of the Songhay language. "The people have great confidence in you, Monsieur Paul," he told me. "They have opened themselves to you. I suppose it can be said that you are retracing the path of Rouch."

The greatest compliment one can receive from the older people in the Songhay countryside is to be compared to Rouch. At the time I was a brash student of the Songhay. I didn't want to be compared to anyone. How could I convince people like Issaka Boulhassane that I wasn't retracing the path of Rouch? Would he ever understand that I had my own research agenda (which was at that time to study Songhay religion from a symbolist rather than a Griaulian perspective? I was interested in the interpretation of significant symbols, not in the exhaustive collection of data that obsessed Griaule. I realize now that "retracing the path of Rouch" in Songhay put me on a road leading to rich ethnographic rewards; it was part of my ethnographic initiation.[7]

Following Rouch's path, the path of the Songhay spirits, brought me to Adamu Jenitongo, the sorcerer and possession priest of Tillaberi. After I became Adamu Jenitongo's apprentice, people in Tillaberi began to call me *Anasara zima*, "the European possession priest." People who knew me better called me *sohanc'izo*, "the son of a *sohanci*," and even *Jenitongo hama*, "the grandson of Jenitongo," a famous sorcerer from the Ouallam region of Niger, some 100 kilometers due east of Tillaberi, who was the father of Adamu.

In 1981 I saw Rouch and told him about being temporarily paralyzed in Wanzerbé.[8]

"You are making progress," he told me. "You must continue year after year. You are following the right path."

We made arrangements to meet Boubou Hama, the Nigerien historian and former President of the National Assembly of Niger during the regime of Hamani Diori (1960–74). Even Boubou Hama had heard of my progress on Rouch's path. He addressed me as *zima kayna*, "the little possession priest." Rouch, of course, was *zima beri*, "the big possession priest."

How amusing are the marvels of fictive kinship, of human classification. All too often, ethnographers are so busy classifying others that we don't take time to explore how the others classify us. You are my "brother"; you are my "cross-cousin"; you are my "son"; you are my "daughter"; you are "the European"; you are my "father"; you are "Monsieur Claude's daughter."

In 1984 I learned what it fully meant to walk in the Nigerien shadow cast by the myth of Jean Rouch. A colleague of mine had been to Simiri, a village where Rouch had filmed many possession ceremonies over the years. I had not been to Simiri, but the people there, especially Daouda Sorko, the Simiri possession priest, knew that I was following Rouch's path. Daouda Sorko knew that I had learned much about possession and sorcery from Adamu Jenitongo. My colleague was astounded that they knew so much about me.

"Do you know what they call you in Simiri?" she asked me.

"No."

"They call you *Rouch'izo*," which translates to "son of Rouch," "little Rouch," or "Rouch's seed."

SONGHAY IMAGES OF THE ETHNOGRAPHER

This account of "Rouch'izo," of course, is my creation. It was created through the dialectic of my experience of a few Songhay and their experience of me in the context of contemporary times. The issue of the mutuality of field experience is not a new one in anthropology. It was first fully bridged in Rabinow's pioneering *Reflections on Fieldwork in Morocco* and underscored in Dumont's *The Headman and I* and Riesman's *Freedom in*

Fulani Social Life. These and other monographs and articles have discussed fully the contingent nature of the field experience and the importance of interpretation to the ethnographic enterprise.[9]

What were the contingencies that drove people to categorize me? So far I have discussed how a small number of people called me Rouch'izo, Anasara Zima, or Sohanc'izo. Many of my age-mates called me *baso*, or "cross-cousin," which gave them license to insult me ritually with such pithy barbs as "Your father's penis," or "Your mother's vagina." A few people called me "my son," or "my brother," fully expecting me to meet various filial obligations. Sometimes this fictive kinship was felt genuinely; most times it was the means to the end of money. "He's taking advantage of us," people would say, "why shouldn't we take advantage of him?"

But this is only a small part of my story, for most of the Songhay with whom I came in contact did not know me personally; they simply called me *Anasara*, "the European." The term Anasara is borrowed from the Arabic *nazareen*, or Christian. Over the years the word has become synonymous with "white man." And so most of the Songhay I met categorized me as "the white man." People would come up to me and say, "How are you today, Anasara?"; or "Where are you traveling today, Anasara?"; or simply, "Anasara, good day." The children even got into the act. They would walk up to me and say, "Anasara, cadeau [gift]"; or if they had learned a smattering of French, "Anasara bonjou, donne-moi 5 francs" (European, good day. Give me 5 francs). Some of the smaller children never uttered a word; they simply approached me and held out their open palms.

No one likes to be treated insensitively, and my retort to these mercenary greetings was an appropriate proverb, *"Iri koy ma dogonaandi"* (May Allah lighten your burden), to which the interlocuter must respond, "Amen." Sometimes I would complain to the adults that I was not the bank, an endless source of money. "Why don't you ask the merchants in town for money?" I would urge them. There were many merchants, in fact, whose daily income far outdistanced my humble monthly stipend. Many of these men wore exquisite robes; some of them owned trucks. "Ask the merchants for money," I would say.

"But they won't give us anything," the able-bodied beggars would respond.

These sorts of incidents are nothing new to anthropologists. But how many of us make them a subtext in our ethnographic writings? What do they reveal?

THE CONSTRUCTION OF ANASARA-SONGHAY CATEGORIES

In my case, Songhay categorizations of me led to an investigation of the historical basis for the construction of Songhay categorizations of the

European. My experience thrust me into the constructionist literature, which is nicely summarized by Sandra Scarr.

All the world's a stage, but the script is not *As You Like It*, it is *Rashomon*. Each of us has our own reality in which we try to persuade others. Facts do not have an independent existence. Rather, facts are created within theoretical systems that guide the selection of observations and the invention of reality.[10]

Specific historical and political events have created a set of European images of Africa and Africans. Likewise, specific historical and political events have created a set of African images of Europe and European (i.e., whites).

In Niger the conditions that framed the Anasara-Songhay relationship existed long before I set foot in Mehanna in August of 1976. The first contact between Europeans and Songhay-speaking populations probably occurred during the ill-fated adventure of René Caillé in the early part of the nineteenth century. We know that shortly thereafter Songhay people came in contact with Heinrich Barth. These men were on fact-finding missions and have left us with detailed descriptions of life in the Sahel in the early and middle nineteenth century. But the contact between these explorers and Songhay people was not at all systematic. At that time Songhay polities were independent and their chiefs enjoyed full authority over their peoples. It was not until the very end of the nineteenth century that systematic and fully politicized relations developed between Songhay and European. During this period French military expeditions, including the infamous Voulet-Chanoine mission in 1899, conquered easily all of what had been Songhay country. After the Voulet-Chanoine mission had massacred 400 people in the Songhay village of Sasane-Hausa, it was easy for the French to establish both their garrisons and their rule in the middle Niger valley.[11] And so the first attribute in the Anasara-Songhay relationship was established: Europeans conquer, which implies massacre followed by governance. It also granted the European superior status in the dyadic relationship—a status Europeans took great pains to maintain.

The second attribute in the Anasara-Songhay relationship was systematic cultural humiliation, a tactic which the European applied to convince the African of his savage inferiority—and of the European's civilized superiority. For example, in 1901 William Ponty, the Governor-General of French West Africa, abolished slavery in the French Sudan. This act reduced the social importance of slavery in Songhay regions. Since slavery was the principal foundation of the pre-colonial social order, the abolition of this practice undermined significantly the authority of Songhay chiefs.[12] By 1908 French colonial officials estimated that some 200,000 slaves in the

Western Sudan had left their masters. In 1911 Governor-General Ponty suggested that 500,000 slaves had liberated themselves.[13]

The European education policy also sought to undermine Songhay cultural and political autonomy by producing a new elite educated in the French language and culture. The members of this literate elite would become the bulwark of the colonial administration—the clerks.

Although there were a few movements of resistance to French colonial rule, the colonial armies quickly squelched these doomed uprisings. And so the Anasara collected taxes from Songhay, forced young Songhay to build roads, and conscripted young Songhay men into the Armed Forces.[14] Meanwhile, the Anasara lived well his European life in the growing cities of Niamey and Tillaberi. He had cars, butter, more meat than he could eat, and servants whom he paid to wait on him. The Anasara had an endless supply of money and power; most Songhay had limited wealth and no power.

The fallout of the asymmetrical power dynamic that existed between Songhay and European led to the construction of stereotypes. We are all familiar with our labels of Africans. Created within frameworks established in the eighteenth and nineteenth centuries, Europeans associated Africans—and still do in large measure—with fetishism, heathenism, cannibalism, savagery, barbarism, and idolatry.[15] For example,

> the cause of idolatry is that man, through sin, left behind the contemplation of the divine, invisible, and intellectual nature and sank wholly into the senses, with the result that he is incapable of being touched by objects other than objects of the senses; hence he has come to the forgetfulness of God and worships stars, elements, animals, even images, passions, and vices, and finally, everything other than God.[16]

These stereotypic labels, of course, correspond to certain behavioral expectations: interminable laziness, uncontrolled sensuality, and irremediable stupidity.

The fallout of the Anasara-Songhay relationship also led to the less publicized African stereotypes of Europeans. Through the plastic arts and through ritual frames, Africans mocked their European rulers. The Igbo erected *Mbari* houses in the bush. These structures house statues that burlesque strangers, most of whom are Europeans.[17] In the Yoruba *gelede* cult, one group of dancers wear *ouibo* masks consisting of long, straight monkey hair, long noses, and eye-glasses. Dressed formally as ballroom dancers, they work in the audience, saying "How do you do?"[18] In Songhay there is the Hauka family of possession deities, all of whom burlesque the colonial order. There are such deities as *Gomno*, the Governor-General, *Zeneral Malia*, the General of the Red Sea, and *King Zuzi*, the colonial Chief Justice.[19] The Hauka cult is a veritable theater of cultural resistance, a stage on which Songhay mercilessly mock their Anasara counterparts. Through time, then, there was established and reinforced a mythology about the Anasara: he was rich; he was racist; he cared only for himself; he ate pork.

The Anasara attributes have survived the transition from colonialism to independence. There remains today a stereotypic Anasara. In times of scarcity, drought, and famine it is the Anasara who provides life-saving grain, a fact that reinforces the ongoing image of Anasara power and wealth. Despite an independent government in Niger, there are many teams of Anasara experts—technicians, agricultural and livestock scientists—who work on "development projects." Like the Anasara of the colonial period, these people live in fine houses, own cars, and hire servants.

The reason that these Anasara attributes are still important today stems from the rapport of individual Songhay to their history. For most Songhay history is a living tradition. Just as the identities of such mythic culture heroes as Sonni Ali Ber are dramatized during possession ceremonies, so the images of the Anasara are reinforced through the Hauka family of Songhay deities. For most Songhay, then, history is not bound up in texts; it is a foundation of ongoing social relations.

And so, when I began my fieldwork in 1976, people in Mehanna had a pre-ordained set of assumptions about me: I was rich; I was racist; I cared only for myself; I ate pork. Younger people considered me one of the many tourists who breeze through Songhay villages after having crossed the Sahara.

The point of this exposition, of course, is that what we make of Songhay or any other group of people is contingent. Whom do we meet? Do they accept us? Do they tell the whole truth and nothing but the truth? And what does truth-telling, whatever that is, depend upon? Is it a matter of interpersonal chemistry? Is it a matter of how the ethnographer fits into the always already world of the field? Is it a matter of a socioeconomic situation conditioned by world-wide socioeconomic and political forces?[20]

The premises of constructionism attempt to answer these questions of contingency.

> If one adopts . . . a constructionist position on epistemology, then knowledge of all kinds, including scientific knowledge, is a construction of the human mind. Sensory data are filtered through the knowing apparatus to the human senses and made into perceptions and cognitions. The human mind is also constructed in a social context, and its knowledge is in part created by the social and cultural context in which it comes to know the world.[21]

In short, social or scientific facts are not discovered; they are, as Wagner has eloquently told us, "invented."[22] More profoundly, facts are "invented" in contexts in which thought, action, and feeling are inseparable—all part of our fully lived experience.[23]

THE PARADOX OF KNOWLEDGE/POWER

Jean Rouch did much of his ethnographic work when Niger was still a French colony. Son of Rouch—me—has done all of his work in the independent Republic of Niger. When Rouch did his early formative work, most Songhay lived in grass huts. Songhay who traveled did so by means of their feet, donkey, horse, camel, or dugout. When I landed in Mehanna in 1976, most of the village consisted of mudbrick houses, and most people traveled by means of truck, bush taxi, or motorized dugout. Mehanna was not an isolated example. In what was once the isolated bush of Rouch's era, there are now hundreds of radios. Since the news is broadcast in the five major languages of Niger, people in remote areas can be informed about world and national affairs. In 1977 people in Mehanna knew about the fast-flying Concorde, economic difficulties in Europe, and the record-setting cold wave in the United States. In recent years, the Government of Niger has set up a national television network. In the larger towns each neighborhood chief has a receiver in his compound. Every evening, the time when the daily broadcasts begin, people from the neighborhood crowd into the chief's compound to watch television. The broadcasts consist of a news program in several languages, programs about the cultural traditions of Niger, local theater, and documentary and feature films—including, of course, Jean Rouch films. In the major hardware store of Niamey, the capital of Niger, there is a "videothèque," frequented by Anasara and Nigeriens alike, from which one can rent video cassettes of the latest French and American films.

The difference between the technological innovations of the era of Rouch and that of "son" of Rouch is that the information revolution of the contemporary age has seemingly altered the status of knowledge. During the past forty years, according to Lyotard, knowledge has been exteriorized.

> The old principle that the acquisition of knowledge is indissociable from the training of minds, or even individuals is becoming obsolete and will become ever more so. . . . Knowledge is and will be produced in order to be sold, it is and will be consumed in order to be valorized in a new production: in both cases, the goal is exchange.[24]

If one accepts Lyotard's argument, there is no noble savage in the world of late consumer society. Noble savages have long had access to knowledge— the means to information. Increasingly, these citizens of the "peripheral states" are gaining access to the technology needed to produce knowledge—the means to sell information.[25]

But has the information revolution had an impact on the perceptions of Africans? Despite the aura of change, much has remained the same. The ever-powerful discourse of the marketplace still reinforces nineteenth-century racist myths about Africa. Contemporary travel brochure writers, for example, paint a picture of Togo not far removed from the discourse of the late nineteenth-century travel writers:[26]

> Togo is just a slice of country, never more than 100 miles in width and only 360 miles long. Its diminutive boundaries belie a cultural and geographic diversity, and can mislead those who underestimate its influence. Togo is the homeland of voodoo. We are continually surrounded here by this religion that is based on sorcery and the spiritual power of charms and fetishes.[27]

This kind of advertising copy is read by thousands of would-be tourists as they contemplate a trip to Africa.

The persistent popularity of writer V. S. Naipaul has also reinforced nineteenth-century African myths of "darkness and mystery."[28] Echoing Joseph Conrad, Naipaul writes in his "The Crocodiles of Yamoussoukro":

> The feeding ritual takes place in the afternoon, in bright light. There are cars, the tourists in bright clothes, the cameras. But the crocodiles are sacred. A live offering—a chicken—is often made to them; it is part of the ritual. This element of sacrifice, this protracted display of power and cruelty, is as unsettling as it is meant to be, and it seems to bring *night* and *forest* close again to the dream of Yamoussoukro.[29] (my emphasis)

How many of Naipaul's readers will have the intellectual curiosity to consult anthropological texts on the religious practices of societies in the Ivory Coast? How many of Naipaul's readers will recognize the superficiality of his text?

If European myths about Africans are stubbornly persistent, so too are Songhay myths about Europeans. Throughout Songhay, knowledge about the Anasara has increased exponentially during the past twenty years, yet Songhay categorizations about Europeans, including myself, have changed little. The living tradition of Songhay history will not be overcome by the superficial imagery of the information revolution.[30]

There is only a small group of Songhay who know Jean Rouch personally. Few Songhay would recognize Rouch if they saw him in the flesh. What most Songhay know is the myth of Jean Rouch, the European who went to Wanzerbé, the white man who "follows the spirits."

Although the myth of Jean Rouch is important in Songhay, the forces of history, politics, and international economics make the myth insignificant to daily life. In conversations that I have had in Songhay over a period of nineteen years, the subject of Jean Rouch has surfaced only in highly specific contexts: talk of sorcery, witchcraft, or possession. Rouch, and "son" of Rouch, for that matter, are minor topics of philosophical rumination. In my experience, most Songhay lump Europeans into a single homogeneous category: Anasara. And so anthropologists in Songhay are frequently mistaken for tourists, diplomats, or technical consultants.

It is not surprising that these kinds of classificatory incidents occur. Most anthropologists are all too familiar with them. We never get to know everybody in the field. Many of the people among whom we live, as a consequence, may ignore us as individuals. But conditions of history, economics, and politics force "them" to confront what "we" represent. To "them," what we represent is sometimes hilarious; it is often ugly, oppressive, or embarrassing; it is usually beyond our control to shape or change.

My point, of course, is that reports of embarrassing classificatory incidents rarely find their way into anthropological texts. If we give others as much of a voice as the anthropologists reserve for themselves, our writing will reflect faithfully the epistemological, historical, and political contexts of our investigations. Besides, these reports will infuse our texts with humor and shield our readers from the "dead hand of competence."

PART III

Sounds in Cultural Experience

Toute pour l'oeil, Rien pour l'oreille

Baudelaire

6 | *Sound in Songhay Possession*

One afternoon in 1970 in Tillaberi, the haunting cries of the monochord violin drew me over a dune to witness my first ceremony of Songhay spirit possession. The possession dance was held in the compound of Adamu Jenitongo, who would later become the master my apprenticeship in Songhay sorcery. The sounds of these instruments so impressed me that I continued to attend possession ceremonies in 1971. Upon my return to Niger in 1976 I again listened for the "cries" of the violin and the "clacks" of the gourd drum. In 1977 I began to learn about the sounds of spirit poetry in the village of Mehanna. Two years later, I was invited to join the Tillaberi possession troupe as a "servant to the spirits," with such duties as gathering ritual plants and resins and costuming male mediums. In 1984 the absence of rain threatened the growing season, and in a two-week period in July I participated in ten possession ceremonies during which people begged their spirits to bring rain. That year drought ravaged Tillaberi. Many people died. Throughout this myriad of experiences, my teachers continually focused my attention on the sounds of possession.

"Listen to the *godji* [violin] and let its cries penetrate you. Then you will know the voice of the spirits," they would tell me. "Feel the sound of the drum and know the power of our past." And so I listened and I felt the music, and over time, I began to hear the sounds of Songhay possession.

*   *   *

The eye and its gaze, to use the apt term of Foucault, has had a lockhold on Western thought.[1] In this book, for example, four of the chapters focus on "visions"; "our" visual takes on "them," and "their" visual takes on us. In

Figure 10: Musicians at a possession ceremony in Mehanna, 1977

those chapters, I was concerned primarily with the notion of the "gaze" and its impact on human categorization. In this section, I attempt to disregard the "gaze," and tune into the dimension of sound in two ethnographic domains: Songhay possession ceremonies and Songhay sorcery.

EYE, GAZE, AND TONE

Ever since the period of alphabetization, of which Ong writes so eloquently, sound-in-the-world has been spatialized and the oral-aural world has been relegated to the back benches of philosophical debating chambers.[2] Zuckerkandl suggests that the majesty of vision in the epistemology of Western thought stems from our traditional stress on the observation of material things within a field of vision.[3] From Aristotle on we have been conditioned to see colored illuminated things, not colors or light. We feel hard or smooth things, not hardness or smoothness. "In seeing, touching, tasting, we reach through the sensation to an object, to a thing. Tone is the only sensation not that of a thing."[4] In Western discourse we have tended in our acts of seeing to spatialize the phenomena we observe. Foucault provides a medical example:

> For us the human body defines, by natural right, the space of origin and of the distribution of disease: a space whose lines, volumes, surfaces, and routes are laid down in accordance with a now familiar geometry, by the anatomical atlas. But this order of the solid visible body is only one way—in all neither the first nor the most fundamental—in which one spatializes disease.[5]

Western thinkers have generally ignored the dimension of sound.[6] For Zuckerkandl, sound can be organized into melodies, rhythms, meters, and most of all into forces. The meaning of a sound "lies not in what it points to, but in the pointing itself."[7] He considers the sounds of music as dynamic symbols: "We hear forces in them as the believer sees the divine being in the [religious] symbol."[8] Zuckerkandl's musical view of the universe presents for us an entry into the world of intangibles: "Because music exists, the tangible and visible cannot be the whole of the given world, something we encounter, something to which we respond."[9] With our ears fully tuned to the existential nature of sound, we can better appreciate the intangible and can cross thresholds into the deep recesses of a people's experience. Feld demonstrates this very point. In his book on Kaluli sound as a cultural system, he shows that

> By analyzing the form and performance of weeping, poetics, and song in relation to their origin myth and the bird world they metamorphize, Kaluli sound expressions are revealed as embodiments of deeply felt sentiments.[10]

In Songhay, sound is more than a means to the end of trance; it is a foundation of experience.[11] If one cannot hear, Sorko Djibo Mounmouni once suggested to me, one can learn little about the world. A deeper appreciation of sound could force us to overturn our static, spatialized world and consider the dynamic nature of sound, an open door to the comprehension of cultural sentiment.

POSSESSION IN SONGHAY

The whine of the violin (*godji*), the syncopated "clack" of the gourd drum, the roar of the deities, and the murmur of the audience have long echoed in the dry air above Songhay villages. Possession ceremonies, which probably date to the reign of Askia Mohammed Touré, are a major component of Songhay religion.[12] They are ceremonies in which visions and sounds are fused to re-create Songhay experience from mythic past to realistic present.

Possession and the Cosmos

According to Adamu Jenitongo, the Songhay world consists of seven heavens, seven hells, and earth, on which there are four cardinal directions. There are also two elementary domains on earth: the world of social life and the world of eternal war, the spirit world. God lives in the most distant, seventh heaven. Since God is so distant, contact with him comes only through the good offices of *Ndebbi*, God's messenger, who inhabits the sixth heaven. Priests chant their magical incantations to Ndebbi, who then carries the message to God for a decision. Songhay elders are divided about which members of the spirit family reside in heavens two through five. Some elders, including Adamu Jenitongo, suggest that these heavens house the ancestors; others maintain that these heavens are the abode of angels. The first, most proximate heaven is the domain of the spirits or *holle*, which are divided into the following spirit "families":

1. *The Tooru:* the nobles of the spirit world that control such natural forces as the wind, the clouds, the Niger River, fire, lightning, and thunder. Some Tooru are considered Songhay; others represent neighboring ethnic groups: Gurmantche, Tuareg, Bella, Hausa.

2. *The Genji Kwari:* the "White Spirits," which are the Islamic clerics and dispute arbitrators of the social and spirit worlds (white being the color worn by Islamic clerics). Some of these are thought to be Songhay; many are thought to be Tuareg.

3. *The Genji Bi:* the "Black Spirits," identified as "Voltaiques" (Moose, Gurmantche, Kurumba), that control the forces governing soil fertility and pestilence. As the original inhabitants of Songhay, they are the masters of the earth.

4. *The Hargay:* "the Spirits of the Cold." Identified with Songhay, Fulan, and Bella (neighboring ethnic groups), these spirits govern illness, especially those associated with reproduction.

5. *The Hausa Genji (Doguwa):* the spirits associated exclusively with the

Hausa-speaking peoples of eastern Niger and northern Nigeria. They precipitate madness and various kinds of paralysis.

6. *The Hauka:* the Spirits of Force that represent identities in French colonial society.[13]

Each family represents, moreover, a period of Songhay experience. The Tooru, the most ancient of the spirit families, probably date back to Askia Mohammed Touré, and are associated with the religion practiced by the *don borey,* the people of the past. The Genji Kwari, too, date from Askia's time. They represent the widespread Islamization during the imperial period. Conquering Songhay armies in the fourteenth, fifteenth, and sixteenth centuries vanquished Voltaique populations (Gurmantche, Moose, and Kurumba), the first inhabitants of Songhay (in what is today the Republic of Niger), represented by the Genji Bi. The Hargay and Hausa spirits are more recent phenomena. The Hargay are spirits of recently deceased people who were highly renowned for their social deviance. The Hausa came to Songhay with Hausa-speaking merchants who migrated west in the early part of the twentieth century. The Hauka, for their part, represent the colonial age. Each spirit family, then, signifies a distinct historical period during which there occurred a sociocultural crisis.

The proximity of social and spirit domains parallels a resemblance between spirits and human beings. Like human beings, spirits are members of various ethnic groups, marry one another, and have master-slave relationships. Unlike human beings, the spirits are invisible and live forever.[14]

The juxtaposition of the first heaven and earth also creates in the world two contiguous domains: the world of social life and the world of the spirits. These worlds are fused during possession ceremonies, when the spirits leave their world—the first heaven—to visit the social world by taking a medium's body: the fusion of the worlds.

Spirit mediumship results from the temporary displacement of a person's double by the force of a particular spirit. When the force of the spirit enters the medium's body, the person shakes uncontrollably. When the deity's double is firmly established in the dancer's body, the shaking becomes less violent. The deity screams and dances. The medium's body has become a deity.

Possession ceremonies are not everyday happenings in Songhay communities. During the rainy season (June to November) people are too busy with farm work to engage frequently in possession activities; the peak of the possession season is toward the end of the long dry season. From April to the beginning of June the *zimas,* or possession priests, organize the farming and rain possession ceremonies which they believe are necessary for successful agriculture.

Zimas also stage ceremonies to protect the community, to resolve individual problems, to ensure a farmer's good crop, and to mourn or protect members of the possession troupe. Most possession ceremonies are organized to meet the needs of individuals in the community. Ceremonies are held, for example, to ask the advice of the spirits about an upcoming marriage. A woman who has suffered a miscarriage or a stillbirth may ask a zima to organize a ceremony to beckon *Nya Beri* (literally, "great mother"). Nya Beri is the mother of the Cold Spirits that bring on these horrors.

Possession ceremonies for community protection are relatively infrequent. In 1971 village elders along the Niger River asked the zimas to organize possession ceremonies to protect their communities from a cholera epidemic. In 1983 and 1984 officials of the Nigerien Government asked priests in Tillaberi, the site of my field research, to organize a series of possession ceremonies to bring rain to the drought-ravaged lands. In some Songhay-speaking communities, the chief's installation is celebrated with a possession ceremony. The spirits come to the social world to greet the new chief. They also ask him for gifts. In this way the chief assures the polity of his allegiance to the spirit world and to the ancestors.

Three possession ceremonies are tied to farming activities. The first of these is called the Black Spirit Festival (*genji bi hori*). The zimas stage this ceremony in April to pay homage to the spirits of the land which control soil fertility and various forms of pestilence. If the ceremony is successful, Adamu Jenitongo explained, the millet crop will be protected from rats, birds, and insects.

The second farming ceremony is the *yenaandi* or rain dance, which is a re-enactment of the first possession ceremony that took place in the ancestral past, and is still staged in most Songhay villages. In the rain dance, priests call to the social world four (or more) principal Tooru deities: Dongo, deity of thunder; Cirey, deity of lightning; Moussa Nyori, deity of clouds and wind; and Hausakoy, deity of iron-smithing. If the rain dance is well staged, the spirits are pleased and the community is assured of enough rain to produce a bountiful harvest.

Zimas organize a third farming ceremony after the harvest, called "eating the new millet." At this, a celebration of thanksgiving held by the possession troupe, the spirits are invited to sample the new millet.

The Possession Troupe

In many Songhay villages there is a loosely organized group of men and women who constitute the local possession troupe. These men and women gather periodically to stage possession ceremonies. The head of the Songhay troupe is the aforementioned zima or possession priest. Like the impressario of a theatrical company, the zima produces possession ceremonies in Songhay. He makes sure that the proper sacrificial animals have

Figure 11: A possession ceremony in Mehanna, 1977

been purchased. He hires musicians and praise-singers. He requires the attendance of spirit mediums. But the zima is more than a producer. During ceremonies he directs the ritual action, orchestrating musical arrangements, overseeing costume changes, and interpreting spirit language. He is also responsible for the distribution of money that the troupe collects during a ceremony.

If the zima is the head of the Songhay spirit possession troupe, the medium is its heart. Spirits invade the bodies of their mediums to speak to people in Songhay communities. Although the majority of mediums in Songhay are women, a large percentage are men. Contrary to much of the literature on possession, Songhay mediums come from all the social strata in the Republic of Niger.[15] Despite their social divergence, mediums in Songhay share a number of social and experiential bonds. First, mediumship is passed down through the kindred. If a person's close relative is a spirit medium, he or she is likely to inherit one of that medium's spirits. Second, spirits mark their mediums by making them sick. The prepossession maladies are cured through initiation into the troupe. Third, each medium, through his or her initiation, is linked perpetually to the spirit world. No matter their accomplishments in the social world, mediums are obliged to pay lifelong homage to the spirits. They are also required to support directly or indirectly the activities of spirit possession troupes.

The cast of the Songhay possession troupe is completed by its praise-singers (sorkos), and musicians. Sorkos are descendants of Faran Maka Bote, a legendary Niger River fisherman who may have lived during the tenth century. Son of Nisile Bote, also a fisherman, and Maka, a river genie, Faran was the first human being to control the spirits of the Niger River. In Faran's time the spirits rendered themselves visible to human eyes. They revealed some of their secrets to Faran, who used them to control the Niger River. Before they reverted to their invisibility they taught Faran their praise-poetry and music. They said to Faran:

"If they play this music and recite these words, we will reappear in the bodies of dancers."

Soon thereafter Faran staged the first possession ceremony, a rain rite which he called *yene* ("to cool off"). Patrilineal descendants of Faran, sorkos, learn today the sacred praise-poetry of their ancestor, the poetry of the spirits of the Songhay pantheon. Sometimes sorkos become zimas. Usually, however, they restrict themselves to praise-singing at possession ceremonies, and to their role as healers.

There are two kinds of musicians who perform at spirit possession ceremonies in Songhay: monochord violinists and gourd drummers. Often, the musicians learn their art as apprentices to close relatives: father, father's brothers, mother's brothers. Sometimes a spirit will "appoint" a musician, who may be simply a member of a possession audience.[16] Sometimes, musicians are also spirit mediums, zimas, and sorkos. The most illustrious monochord violinist was Wadi Godji, who died in the 1950s. Besides playing his monochord violin in Simiri, Wadi Godji was also a sorko and a zima in the local possession troupe.

SOUND IN SONGHAY POSSESSION

Anthropological writers have long discussed the meaning of words in cultural life. From Malinowski to Tambiah, anthropologists have attempted to explain the magical power of incantations from a variety of perspectives. Rarely, however, have these analysts focused on the importance of the sound of words (see Chapter 7). Rarer still are analyses of the importance of the sound of musical instruments. In the remainder of this chapter, I shall describe the importance of both the sound of musical instruments and the sound of praise-poetry in Songhay possession.

The Sound of the Godji

The sound of the *godji*, or monochord violin used by Songhay musicians during possession ceremonies, corresponds to deep themes in Songhay experience. The resonating cavity of the godji consists of one-half of a hard gourd which has been cut along the axis of its grain. The opening of the resonating cavity is parallel to the neck of the violin, and its diameter averages about 29 cm.[17] The gourd of the violin is covered by a lizard skin, *bo (Varanus niloticus)* which is stretched over the opening of the gourd and fastened to the instrument with either small iron nails or the thorns of the *garbey* tree (*Balinites aegytica*). The neck of the instrument is a simple stick of wood carved from the *kubu* tree (*Combretum micrantum*); it is generally 75 cm in length. The neck is inserted into the resonating cavity about 3 cm below the point where the gourd was cut into two halves. The violin string consists of black hair clipped from a horse's tail; it is tied to the end of the neck and to a piece of wood attached at the far end of the resonating cavity. The musician pulls the string taut as he pushes a small wooden bridge into position. The bow is an arc of wood to which is attached more black hair clipped from a horse's tail.[18]

When the musician plays the godji he produces a sound that is quite high in pitch—similar to a high-pitched wail. Indeed, in Songhay one says that the godji "cries" (*a ga he*). As Adamu Jenitongo told me: "The godji cries for me; it cries for you; it cries for the people of Tillaberi; it cries for all the Songhay."[19]

Because the godji "cries" for all the Songhay, it is the most sacred of instruments. It was the prize given to Faran Maka Bote when he vanquished the river genie Zinkibaru to gain control of the Niger River spirits. Considering its mythic history, the godji and its sound are said to link Songhay of the present and past. Indeed, the godji is so sacred that it should never be played on nonsacred occasions. Generally, it is kept in a cloth sack and is placed in a zima's sacred spirit house, a hut in which a zima keeps his or her sacred objects.

The godji is more than an instrument with a sound that links the Songhay with their ancestors. As Adamu Jenitongo said:

> The sound of the godji penetrates and makes us feel the presence of the ancestors, the ancients [*don borey*]. We hear the sound and know that we are on the path of the ancestors. The sound is irresistible. We cannot be unaffected by it and neither can the spirits, for when they hear it "cry," it penetrates them. Then they become excited and swoop down to take the body of the medium.[20]

The sound of the godji is a tangible link between Songhay present and past, for this wailing sound revivifies deep-seated cultural themes about the nature of life and death, the origin of Songhay, the juxtaposition of the social and spirit worlds. These themes, in turn, reinforce Songhay cultural identity.

The Sound of the Gasi

The *gasi*, or gourd drum, is also a Songhay instrument of unquestioned sacredness. Like the godji, it is played only during possession ceremonies. Although much larger than the gourd used for the godji, the hard gourd used for the gasi is also cut into two halves along the axis of its grain. When the musician wishes to play his gasi, he digs a hole in the sand at the edge of the possession dance ground. When the ground is overturned and placed over the hole, the drum's resonating cavity is deepened considerably. The gourd is stabilized over the hole by a notched stick which the musician extends from under the place where he sits to a point beyond the edge of the gourd. He strikes the drum with a set of carved bamboo sticks which resemble the human hand; in fact, the various parts of the drumstick are called the "wrist" (where the musician grips the drumstick), the "palm" (where the five pieces of bamboo are tied to the "wrist"), and the "fingers" (which when manipulated can strike the drum independently). If the musician strikes the drum with the "wrist" or the "palm," one hears a solid "clack" which echoes in the air. If the musician rolls his own wrist, the "fingers" of the drumstick hit the drum independently, producing a "roll." In this way musicians playing the gasi produce a highly distinctive "clack" and "roll." The ratio of "clacks" to "rolls" corresponds not only to dance movements but to the spirit in the Songhay pantheon which the zima is soliciting.

Like the godji, the gasi appears in Songhay myth. The drum was played originally by river spirits which danced to its beat. The importance of the drum, be it a gasi or a *tourou* (a long slit drum used by Songhay possession musicians in the nineteenth century), is that it produces a highly charged sound which, like the godji, revivifies the ancestral past. Adamu Jenitongo told me that drums were played for the great warriors of Songhay to render them invincible to their enemies. "The sound of the drum explodes from the gasi and reminds us of the ancients and their strength." And so the sound of this special drum—its "clack" and "roll"— intoxicates the dancers as they participate in the possession ceremony, a rite of ancestral origin. The drum sound, like that of the godji, also excites the spirits, creating for them a context in sound which they find irresistible.

The Sound of Praise-Poetry

In the western Sahel of Africa the social-symbolic importance of praise-poetry—and the people who produce it—is widespread. Bards (*griots*) have played major roles in the histories of the great empires of the western Sudan (Ghana, Mali, Songhay). In the epic poetry of these empires, "griots appear as spokesmen and advisors to kings, preceptors for princes, genealogists for families and clans, composers, singers and musicians who perform for all segments of society."[21] Bards, in fact, continue to play important roles in the nation-states of the contemporary western Sahel. In the Republic of Niger, for example, the late President Kountché traveled with a number of bards who recited praise-poetry not only about the president's accomplishments but also about the feats of his ancestors. Why has praise-poetry remained so significant in the western Sahel?

Irvine's study of the rhetoric of praise-naming among the Wolof of Senegal provides a significant hypothesis. Praise-naming, she suggests, has a far-reaching "rhetorical effect." People who are named during a bard's performance "are thought to be morally, socially, and even physically transformed by the words that are said."[22] During a praise-naming ceremony among the Wolof, a stratified caste society, the praise-naming increases the addressee's moral standing, augments his rank in a rank-conscious society, and precipitates some kind of physiological transformation. It is believed that these transformations occur because the praise-naming ceremony arouses emotion in the addressee which, in turn, alters the balance of his bodily fluids. According to Wolof theories, these bodily fluids are the biological determinants of social position. The physiological (magical) transformation in the addressee is also influenced by the physical sounds of words.

> Words do not just have meaning—they are breath and vibrations of air, constituted and shaped by the body and motives of the speaker, physically contacting and influencing the addressee. So informants liken the effect of a griot's praise-song on his addressee to the effect of wind upon fire (both metaphorically and literally, since air and fire are supposed to be basic constituents of the body).[23]

Similar ceremonies with similar effects occur throughout the western Sahel. In Songhay the bard's (*jesere*) performance enables people of high rank (nobles or *maigey*) to achieve and maintain high moral, social, and political stature. This stature is achieved and maintained, in part, through the sound of the praise-names in the context of a praise-naming ceremony. It is perhaps because the sounds of the words the bards have mastered carry the power of social, moral and physical (magical) transformation that the bard in the western Sahel continues to maintain his significant social role.

The significance of praise-naming in Songhay extends beyond the political and social domains of life, however. Praise-naming has an essential role in possession ceremonies. The sound of praise-naming has the same impact on Songhay spirits as it seems to have on Songhay addressees. The sorko is the praise-singer to the 150 spirits of the Songhay pantheon. While the godji "cries" and the gasi "clacks" and "rolls" during possession ceremonies, the sorko shouts out the names of the spirits, recounting their genealogies and their supernatural exploits. When the sorko performs his praise-naming, he approaches a spirit medium who is not yet possessed and shouts spirit names into his or her ear. He may even poke the medium's shoulder with his forefinger. These actions, according to Sorko Djibo Mounmouni of Namarigungu (Niger), ensure that the sounds of the praise-names penetrate the medium's body. As in the Wolof case, the sound of the praise-names precipitates a transformation as the spirit, now in a frenzy caused by the sounds of the godji, gasi, and praise-names, takes the body of the medium and throws him or her to the sand. The medium's body is jolted by the paroxysms that mark the onset of possession.

HEARING THE WORLD

Inspired perhaps by Cézanne's notion (and demonstration) that "nature is on the inside," Victor Zuckerkandl tells us that music (and sound, more generally), too, is on the inside; it penetrates us, fusing the material and nonmaterial, the tangible and the intangible.[24] Indeed, Zuckerkandl's thesis on the "inner" dimension of sound merely reaffirms what informants have been telling anthropologists since the beginning of ethnographic field study: that sound is a dimension of experience in and of itself. The Tiv of Nigeria covet song as power, energy, the veritable force of life.[25] For the Dagomba and Ewe of Ghana, music reverberates with power.

> In music, the contrasting, tightly organized rhythms are powerful—powerful because there is vitality in rhythmic conflict, powerful precisely because people are affected and moved. As people participate in a musical situation, they mediate the conflict, and their immediate presence gives power a personal form so that they may relate to it. Thus while people participate with power as a way of relating effectively to each other at a musical or social event, they also participate with power as a religious force. In limiting and focusing Absolute power to specific forms, they encounter power as a reality which is not overwhelming and devastating, but strengthening and upbuilding.[26]

The Kalapalo of central Brazil have a similar musical orientation to the world.

> The mingling of sounds in various situations of performed Kalapalo art is therefore a truly ecological representation of the universe. Through sound symbols, ideas about relationships, activities, causalities, processes, goals, consequences, and states of mind are conceived, represented and rendered apparent to the world. It is through sound that cosmic entities are rendered into being and represented by the Kalapalo—not as object-types but as beings causing and experiencing action in a veritable musical ecology of spirit.[27]

For the Songhay the "cries" of the monochord violin and the "clacks" of the gourd drum *are* the voices of the ancestors, voices filled with the power of the past, powers-in-sound that can bring rain, eradicate pestilence, and prevent epidemics.

Sound for the Songhay and other peoples around the world is believed to have an existence separate from the domains of human, animal, and plant life. Sounds carry forces which are not only good to think, but good to feel.

7 | Sound in Songhay Sorcery

It was in the village of Mehanna in the Republic of Niger that I learned my first lesson in Songhay hearing. I had been studying with Djibo Moun-mouni, a village sorko, a healer who uses words as well as magical powders to heal people who are suffering from illness precipitated by natural and supernatural agents. For four days we attended to a man of some 35 years of age who was suffering from an illness that to me had no discernible diagnosis. The patient had been to the local Islamic healer, to the local health unit, to the regional health unit, and to the National Hospital—all to no avail. The man finally returned to Mehanna and called for Sorko Djibo. The man was so weak he could not support his own weight, and he suffered from chronic nausea and diarrhea. As it was a Thursday, a day when the spirits are close to the social world, the time was right for a healing ritual. Sorko Djibo determined that the man was suffering from witchcraft. A witch, known in Songhay as a *cerkaw*, had stolen the man's double and would eat it. If we could not find the double and return it to the man, Sorko Djibo told me, the man would most certainly die.[1]

We went about our work quickly. Sorko Djibo prepared an ablution, a mixture of twigs, perfume, and water with which the man was to bathe. The sorko then recited a ritual text over the ablution to infuse it with the "force" of the heavens.

> I must speak to Ndebbi, and my words must travel until they are heard. Ndebbi was before human beings. He showed the human beings the path. Now human beings are on the path. My road came from the ancestors [my teacher, my teacher's teacher]. Now my path is beyond theirs. The path is war. When there is war, men have thirty points of misfortune; women have forty points of

Figure 12: Sorko Djibo Mounmouni reciting an incantation over a sacrificial chicken

misfortune. A person has many enemies on the path, enemies who will seek him out. The evil witches can search a person out with evil medicine, and a few of them will be overcome. They say that the evil genies will search a person out and a few of them will be overcome. They say that the devil's children will search a person out and a few of them will be overcome, and the spirits of the cold will search a person out, and they too can be mastered. All of them are on the path, some of them can be mastered.[2]

"Wash him," Sorko Djibo told the man's wife, "especially the joints of the body: the ears, nose, and mouth." Sorko Djibo then took me by the hand and led me out of the man's compound. We began our trek up a large dune toward the outskirts of Mehanna. "Now we shall find the man's double," said the sorko. "Follow me."

And so I did, up the crest of the dune where there was a high pile of *duo* (the husk of the millet seed), for it is outside of town that women let the wind separate the husk from the seed. Sorko Djibo walked into the pile of duo and got down on his hands and knees. He sifted through the husks, jumped up and exclaimed: "Wo, wo, wo, wo" (by flapping the palm of his hand over his open mouth).

He turned toward me. "Did you hear it?"

"Hear what?" I asked dumbfounded.

"Did you feel it?"

"Feel what?" I wondered.

"Did you see it?"

"What are you talking about?" I demanded.

Sorko Djibo shook his head in disbelief. He was disappointed that I had not sensed in one way or another the man's double as he, Djibo, had liberated it. He said to me: "You look but you do not see. You touch, but you do not feel. You listen, but you do not hear. Without sight or touch," he continued, "one can learn a great deal. But you must learn how to *hear* or you will learn little about our ways."

SOUNDS, WORDS, AND CULTURAL EXPERIENCE

The notion of the magical word has long been associated with cosmogony. Mythmakers and scholars alike have grappled with the preeminence of the word. Tambiah suggests that in *Totem and Taboo* Freud was speculating that the deed preceded the word.[3] Linguistic philosophers, by contrast, have suggested that the word is deed. The elegant arguments of Austin and Searle on performative utterances certainly lend some credence to this position.[4] Taking the anthropological perspective, Tambiah reminds us of Goethe's view of the chicken-and-egg question concerning the word and the deed. In *Faust*, the protagonist progresses "from word to thought, then to the notion of power, and [ends] with deed."[5] None of these philosophical ruminations, however, solves the problem Tambiah raises: when a person is asked why a particular ritual or magic rite is effective, he or she invariably answers, "The power is in the words."

Malinowski, among others, paid considerable attention to the relationship between words and magic. He was convinced, in fact, that for the Trobriander the very essence of magic was the spell: "Each rite is the production of force and the conveyance of it, directly or indirectly, to a certain given object, which, as the natives believe, is affected by this force."[6] Malinowski's notion of force was not one of some external energy of supernatural origin; rather, it was an outgrowth of his pragmatic view of language, in which the force of an utterance stems from the reproduction of its consequences, a force which Austin calls "perlocutionary."[7]

Malinowski's contextual ethnographic theory of the language of magic was a major contribution; Tambiah refines Malinowski's view by conjoining word and deed. He writes that language

> ingeniously conjoins the expressive and metaphorical properties of language with the operational and empirical properties of technical activity. It is this which gives magical operations a "realistic" coloring and allows them to achieve their expressiveness through verbal substitution and transfer combined with an instrumental technique that imitates practical action.[8]

In essence, Tambiah attempts to explain the power of words through a description of their sociolinguistic mechanics. Such an analysis is fine, but it presents us with little more than a cursory look at the force of words.

Perhaps one reason for Tambiah's reluctance to enter into the existential space of magical words is that he views magic and the world from the vantage of what Foucault called the classical episteme: words are objectified; they become neutral objects representing things and/or functions.[9] As a consequence, Tambiah does not take into consideration how differing modes of communication might correspond to differing interpretations of the (magical) word. Ong writes:

> cultures which do not reduce words to space but know them only as aural-oral phenomena, in actuality or in the imagination, naturally regard words as more powerful than do literate cultures. Words *are* powerful. Being powered projections, spoken words themselves have an aura of power. Words in the aural-oral culture are inseparable from action for they are always sound.
>
> In oral-aural cultures it is thus eminently credible that words can be used to achieve an effect such as weapons or tools can achieve. Saying evil things of another is thought to bring him direct physical harm. This attitude toward words in more or less illiterate societies is an anthropological commonplace, but the connection of the attitude with the nature of sound and the absence of writing has not until recently begun to grow clear.[10]

Throughout Africa, and elsewhere in the world, the sounds of words are believed to carry potent powers. The Jelgobe Fulani of Burkina Faso "do not find it necessary to imbue their words with emotion when speaking of painful things. To name pain and suffering in a neutral tone is to master them because words do not escape thoughtlessly but are spoken consciously."[11] Indeed, the everyday speech of the Jelgobe has a power of its own. Among the Dinka it is the spoken invocation "which is said to affect and weaken its object, whether a sacrificial victim or a human enemy."[12] In the Bocage of western France,

> witchcraft is spoken words but these spoken words are power, not knowledge or information.
> To talk in witchcraft is never to inform. Or if information is given it is so that the person who is to kill (the unwitcher) will know where to aim his blows. Informing an ethnographer, that is, someone who has no intention of using this information, is literally unthinkable. For a single word (and only a word) can tie or untie a fate, and whoever puts himself in a position to utter it is formidable.
> In short, there is no neutral position with spoken words: in witchcraft, words wage war.[13]

Words, then, are seen as a kind of energy by many peoples in the world, an energy which should be apprehended in and of itself rather than only as a representation of something. Such is the case among the Songhay of Niger, for whom the sound of words is a foundation of a deep-seated cultural experience.[14]

SOUND IN SONGHAY SORCERY

As has been mentioned in several of the preceding chapters, Songhay has a long, glorious history that dates to the latter part of the eighth century, when the legendary Aliaman Za came to the Niger River and slew a river serpent with his iron spear.[15] Demonstrating his overwhelming "force," Aliaman Za took control of the indigenous people of the river and founded the first Songhay dynasty. In all Songhay myths, whether of the origin of the first Songhay dynasty or of the exploits of Faran Maka Bote, the first sorko, the narratives highlight the culture's hero's control of interconnected resources: sorcery and the words that make sorcery possible. The Songhay myth about Faran Maka Bote's battle with the genie Zinkibaru is a case in point.

> Faran lived in Gao. He had a rice field. Every night Zinkibaru came to the rice fields to play his guitar and the fish of the Niger came and ate Faran's rice. One day Faran went fishing and could find only two hippos. It would be a shame to bring home these small prizes from the river. He called his aide, Santana, and left to fight Zinkibaru. Faran found Zinkibaru on an island at the juncture of

seven rivers. Zinkibaru was playing his guitar and the genies of the river were playing gourd drums and a monochord violin. And as the Tooru river spirits were dancing, Faran said to Zinkibaru: "Give me your guitar." Zinkibaru said: "You will have to fight for it. If you win, you will have my guitar and my Tooru captives. If I win I will take your dugout canoe."

Faran was short and fat and Zinkibaru was tall and thin. The battle went on. Faran came toward Zinkibaru, but Zinkibaru said: "The palm leaf will never capture the hippo." This spell was sufficient enough to overcome Faran, who fell to the ground. Zinkibaru took Faran's canoe and left. Faran returned to his mother's house. He was ashamed. He cried. His mother asked him: "Why are you crying?" Faran explained and his mother said to him: "Faran, you have a big head with nothing in it. To fight a spell you need a counterspell. If Zinkibaru said: 'The palm leaf will never capture the hippo,' you only have to say: 'And if the rays of the sun are in front of the leaf?' "[16]

In his second confrontation with Zinkibaru, Faran won this war of words and took control of the river spirits.

In other Songhay myths the spirits reveal the words of incantations to the ancestors, who teach them to their sons, and their sons to their sons, and so on until the words are passed on to the present time. While myths about sorcery and powerful words are told publicly, the incantations themselves are precious secrets not to be revealed to outsiders. Among those who possess the knowledge of powerful words are the sohanci, the patrilineal descendants of Sonni Ali Ber. Sohancis are specialists in military sorcery; they possess the power to cause or protect soldiers from being wounded from arrows, spears, or bullets. They also know the words which will cause or protect people from life-threatening accidents. Like other Songhay healers, they also have an impressive knowledge of the plants that can be used to heal people of physiological and supernatural disorders. Sorkos, all descendants of Faran Maka Bote, are praise-singers to the spirits of the Songhay pantheon. Sorcerers in their own right, sorkos know the words that can repel witches and the spells of other sorcerers. The zima, or ritual priest, is the impresario associated with the Songhay possession troupe. These men and women know the words that have the force to beckon the spirits from the spirit world to the world of social life. All these practitioners undergo long apprenticeships during which they memorize scores of ritual incantations and learn to apply these special words to the substances they prepare for clients. A substance (a vine, tree bark, a stone or a cowry shell) is without power unless a sohanci, a sorko, or a zima has imbued it with force through words.

The Practice of Sorcery

Sorcery in Songhay can be placed into two general categories: sorcery-with-spirits and sorcery-without-spirits. Sorcery-without-spirits is practiced only by sorkos and sohanci and takes two forms: *dangbeli* and *sambeli*.

Dangbeli involves the use of topical poisons, which, are placed in powdered form on a bed or some other object that the victim is likely to touch. The poison enters the bloodstream through the skin and kills its victim in three days or less. In one case, a sorko publicly insulted a powerful sohanci. The sorko died three days later after having defacated his intestines onto the sand.[17] Some of the poisons cause veins and arteries to burst; in this case the victim bleeds to death.[18] In dangbeli, sorcerers do not use incantations; it is sorcery-without-spirits, and is limited to the most powerful sohancis and sorkos.

Sambeli refers to the "magic arrow." Here the sorcerer recites an incantation which, in effect, shoots in the direction of a victim a metaphoric arrow whose tip is loaded with sickness. If the arrow hits its target, which depends upon the power of the sorcerer, the victim becomes lethargic, nauseous; he or she may experience violent diarrhea. If the victim has protection (i.e. wears a special ring or has eaten special foods), the impact of the sorcery is strong but shortlived. If the arrow is not located and removed from an unprotected victim—most people—he or she will wither away and die a slow, horrible death. Sambeli is rarely practiced today; like dangbeli, it is sorcery-without-spirits, a practice also limited to the most powerful and knowledgeable sohancis and sorkos.

Tengbeli, sorcery-with-spirits, is more widely practiced. In tengbeli, sickness is brought on by the recitation of incantations to specific spirits. The sorcerer is hired by an injured party to punish a victim. Reciting the appropriate incantation to the appropriate spirit, and naming the victim, the sorcerer sends sickness—sometimes death—to the victim. If the sorcerer is powerful, the result is immediate. The victim becomes nauseous, delirious, anxious, partially paralyzed. The victim may shake with palsy. Tengbeli, which utilizes powerful words to precipitate a desired effect, can result in the death of the victim.

The Songhay sorcerers with whom I have studied make no distinction between good magic and bad sorcery: for them, sorcery is neither good nor bad, but simply an affair of power. Men and women who send "sickness" also have the capacity to heal a victim suffering from another's sorcery.[19] There is no good or evil in Songhay sorcery; there is only power and the words that enhance power.

THE SOUND OF WORDS

This brief review of the role of the word in the Songhay universe gives only a surface representation of things Songhay. There is much more. Obviously, one must learn to hear the words of incantations; and this, without doubt, is the most important aspect of a young sorcerer's apprenticeship. Learning to hear is more than transforming the sound contours of a magical incantation into one's own speech, however; it is more than mastering the literal and metaphoric meanings of the narratives. To learn how to hear, the Songhay sorcerer must learn to apprehend the sound of words much as the musician learns to apprehend the sound of music. Just as sound is the central feature of the world of music, so sound is the central feature of the world of sorcery. This world of sound comes to life in a network of forces "that act in obedience to laws whose action in manifest in the action of tonal [sound] events, in the precisely determined relations of tones [sounds] to one another in the norms that govern the course of tonal [sound] motion."[20] While the laws governing sound movement differ from melody to melody, from incantation to incantation, the laws have one thing in common: they are dynamic, referring to "states not objects, to relations betweeen tensions, not to positions between, to tendencies, not to magnitudes."[21] Taking this logical sequence one step further, "the forces that act in the tonal world manifest themselves *through* bodies but not upon bodies."[22] In this sense, a tone or an incantation is not a conveyor of action, as Malinowski would have said; rather it *is* action. The physical manifestation of the word *is* significance, to paraphrase Merleau-Ponty, before it *has* significance.[23]

When a musician or an apprentice Songhay sorcerer learns to hear, he or she begins to learn that sound allows for the interpenetration of the inner and outer worlds, of the visible and the invisible, of the tangible and intangible. A person's spatialized "gaze" creates distance. Sound, by contrast, penetrates the individual and creates a sense of communication and participation. From the musical perspective, the "out-there" is replaced by what Zuckerkandl calls the "from-out-there-toward-me-and-through-me."[24] In this way outer and inner words interpenetrate in a flowing and dynamic universe, a universe in which sound is a foundation. Just as in the world of music, where there is no clear distinction between the material and immaterial worlds, so in the Songhay cosmos there is no discrete boundary between the spirit and social worlds. Zuckerkandl's description of the musical world can be applied directly to the Songhay view of the cosmos:

> It is true that the musical concept of the external world—nature pervaded by immaterial forces, the purely dynamic transcending of the physical, space without distinction of places, time in which past and future co-exist with the present, experience of the world in the mode of participation, the external and inward interpenetrating—much more nearly resembles the magical and mythical ideas of primitive or prehistoric peoples than it does the scientific conceptions of modern man.[25]

This musical view of the external world also corresponds to the theories of modern physics.

And so when Sorko Djibo says that there are invisible forces in the universe and that words carry some of these forces to an intended target, are we to discount him? Are we to discount the possibility that words have power?

TO HEAR OR NOT TO HEAR

The Jelgobe Fulani of Burkina Faso inform us of the "force" of everyday expression. The Dinka of the Sudan say that the invocation has the power to weaken a human enemy. The Trobrianders speak to the force of the spell. The peasants of the Bocage in western France demonstrate how "words wage war." The Wolof of Senegal believe that the sound of praise-names in the context of a ceremony can physiologically transform the addressee.[26] The Tiv covet song as power, energy, the veritable force of life.[27] The Songhay invite us to learn about the "force" of the sounds of words, praise-names, and sacred musical instruments.

As the anthropological record suggests, the peoples whom anthropologists study often invite us to learn how to see, how to think, and even how to hear. Many of us accept these invitations genuinely. And once we decide to follow their paths of wisdom, we leave the comforts of a world in which we are members of an intellectual elite and enter worlds of experience in which our illiterate teachers scold us for our ignorance.

*   *   *

Sorko Djibo had scolded me because of my intellectual inabilities. Why had I not been able to hear the bewitched man's *bia* ("double") as it swooshed by me on its way back to its human counterpart? Exhausted from the frustration of instructing such a dullard, Djibo lapsed into silence as we trudged down the sand dune. After what seemed an endless walk back to the bewitched man's compound, we finally entered his courtyard. To my surprise, and to Djibo's satisfaction, the man was vigorously walking about. He strutted up to Sorko Djibo and lavished him with praise. Somehow, he had regained his strength. Sorko Djibo turned to me and said: "The words were good for this one."

My confusion mounting, we left the man's compound. Sorko Djibo led me to his house so that I might receive my first lesson in Songhay hearing. While I had been learning numerous incantations—instructions on how to think—I had not yet begun to learn to hear. He taught me the following incantation:

> X is in the darkness. In the darkness it sees a rock. And the rock sees the evil witch's genitalia. The lights of the witch flash on and off. But when it [the witch] lifts its torch, it is worthless because now it will fall and fear will escape. Men

will not fear you. Women will not fear you. You will not know your front side from your back side. The darkness will be uplifted.[28]

The referential meaning of this incantation taught me about hearing—that the force of the words of the incantation can incapacitate a witch. The power of the incantation is not in the words as carriers of referential meaning, but in the sounds of the words. "X" is the powerful word that incapacitates the witch by causing it to fall from flight. When the sorko recites the text, the sound waves of the word, "X," and all the other words that constitute the incantation, enter into the night air. Through the darkness the powerful sound waves travel to find a rock which guides the sacred sounds to the witch's genitalia. The sound waves of the incantation penetrate the witch's genitalia and the lights of the witch begin to flash. The witch raises its frightening red torch to scare away the sorko. But it is too late. The witch becomes disoriented and no longer poses a threat to the community. "The darkness is uplifted."

Words are powerful and sounds carry force. It is for these reasons that I present the "X" incantation only in English.

PART IV

The Senses in Anthropology

What can be shown cannot be said.

Wittgenstein

8 | The Reconstruction of Ethnography

I na hay faabu wi i garu a ga naasu
"One kills something thin only to discover that [inside] it is fat."

Songhay proverb

My first month of fieldwork among the Songhay of Niger in 1976–77 was a total failure. Having previously lived among the Songhay, and having learned to speak Songhay, I had few problems adjusting to life in a rural village. Still, I did not know many people of the village of Mehanna. Following the wisdom of the literature on fieldwork, I decided to conduct a survey to get to know my neighbors. Soon after I settled in a small mudbrick house, I designed a questionnaire that would generate, or so I thought, some demographic data. But I did not want to limit my survey only to demographics, as the topic of my research concerned the use of language in local-level politics. I therefore added items to the questionnaire on the use of the various languages spoken in Songhay, which is multilingual. These data on language use and language attitudes, I thought, might provide information on relations between Songhay and non-Songhay groups living in Mehanna. This information on cross-ethnic relations, in turn, would reveal patterns of local-level political processes.

After I designed the twenty-item survey, I conducted a pilot test with ten respondents. None had difficulty answering the questions. Encouraged, I administered the survey to a representative sample of townspeople. As in all things one does with the Songhay, I had to make excruciatingly careful arrangements for the survey's administration. First I contacted the village

Figure 13: Sorko Djibo Mounmouni, master of words

chief, who approved the proposal. But before I surveyed individuals, the chief told me, I should consult with the eight neighborhood chiefs. After a series of long visits with the chiefs, I at last began my survey. Unexpectedly, each interview was so long that I could conduct only six interviews a day. It took me thirty days to complete 180 interviews. As I collected data I began to analyze them, and I discovered that multilingualism was greater than I had anticipated. Moreover, a cursory examination of the language attitude data suggested much cross-ethnic enmity.

Toward the end of the Mehanna survey, I interviewed a shopkeeper named Abdou Kano. Abdou told me that he spoke four languages (Songhay, Hausa, Fulani, and Tamasheq). My work with Abdou completed, I walked next door to interview Mahamane Boulla, who, like Abdou, was a shopkeeper. I asked him how many languages he spoke.

"How many languages does Abdou say he speaks?" he asked me.

"Abdou," I said, "says he speaks four languages."

"Hah! I know for a fact that Abdou speaks only two languages."

"What?" I exclaimed. "How could he lie to me?" I stood up abruptly and strutted over to Abdou's shop.

Abdou smiled and greeted me. "Ah, Monsieur Paul, what would you like to buy today?"

"Abdou," I began firmly, "Mahamane has just told me that you speak only two languages. Is that true?"

Abdou shrugged his shoulders. "Yes, it is true. I speak only two languages: Hausa and Songhay."

"Why did you tell me you spoke four languages?"

Abdou patted me on the shoulder. "What difference does it make?" He glanced skyward. "Tell me, how many languages did Mahamane say he speaks?"

"Mahamane," I answered, "told me that he speaks three languages."

"He can speak Songhay and that is all," Abdou said.

"What?" I exclaimed. Turning red with anger, I stormed back to Mahamane's shop. "Abdou tells me that you speak only one language. But you just told me that you spoke three languages. What is the truth?"

Mahamane smiled at me. "Abdou is telling the truth."

"But how could you lie to me?"

Like Abdou, Mahamane shrugged. "What is the difference?"

I spent the next week frantically consulting the other 178 people whom I had interviewed during the previous month. To my disgust, I discovered that everyone had lied to me, and that the data I had so laboriously collected were worthless.

Any audience of fieldworkers, anthropologists or whatnots, can empathize with my predicament, for I am sure that such incidents are not isolated ones. Informants routinely lie to anthropologists for any number of reasons. "What's the difference?" "We don't know you." "We know you, but we don't trust you." "Since you are too young we cannot tell you the truth (but we are too polite to tell you to go away)."

I was lucky because I discovered early in my fieldwork that people were lying to me; some of us are not so lucky, especially if we do not engage in long term fieldwork. Blessed by more luck, I was fortunate to find an elder willing to advise me on learning about things Songhay.

"You will never learn about us," he told me, "if you only go into people's compounds, ask personal questions, and write down the answers. Even if you remain here one year or two years and ask us questions in this manner, we would still lie to you."

"Then what am I to do?"

"You must learn to sit with people," he told me. "You must learn to sit and listen. As we say in Songhay: "One kills something thin only to discover that [inside] it is fat.""

During the remainder of my first year of fieldwork, and subsequent visits to the lands of the Songhay, I have followed my teacher's advice. I learned to listen to a small number of men, to women, and to children, and as a result I learned something about Songhay culture.

I learned to listen to one woman in particular. Fatouma Seyni had been married three times and, when I first met her, she was, as they say in Songhay, "without husband." She talked to me about her marriages: about her first husband who gave her no money, about her second husband who routinely beat her, and about her last husband who often burned her with cigarettes when she was asleep. Whenever Fatouma talked, I listened. Never did I attempt to "interview" her. She asked me questions about myself. We rarely talked about multilingualism, and we never discussed local politics.

When I returned in 1979–80 and in 1981, I went to visit this woman. On each occasion she would greet me and then recite a litany of sorrows. All the while she observed me, saying much about herself and yet revealing little. In 1982–83, I saw Fatouma once again in the Mehanna market. Since she had squash to sell, I bought one for my dinner. As usual, I gave her a small tip of twenty-five francs (roughly ten cents). Fatouma smiled and told me that I was a kindhearted man. Then she bid me to kneel down close to her.

"Go to one of the shops and bring me a vial of perfume this afternoon, around 5 p.m."

"What for?" I asked dumbfounded.

"Just do it. I will see you later."

Later I bought a small vial of *Bint al Hadash* and trekked up the dune to Fatouma's compound. She was sitting on a straw mat next to her mudbrick house. I gave her the perfume.

"You brought the wrong kind of perfume."

"What kind of perfume was I supposed to bring?"

"You were supposed to bring *Bint al Sudan*. How can I put this in my *baata* [a sacrificial container possessed only by sorcerers]?"

"You have a baata!" I exclaimed, overwhelmed.

"Of course I do."

"But you never told me . . ."

"One never talks of these things, one acts. You see, my father was a sorko and he taught me what he knew."

"I have known you for seven years, and never once did you tell me."

Fatouma nodded. "Those of us who are serious never talk about our abilities, or about our work." She stood up and led me inside her house and showed me the baata on her sacrificial altar. She turned to me: "I don't know if the one in the sky [a name for Dongo, spirit of thunder] will accept my putting this perfume in the baata. But I'll do it anyway."

She opened the baata and placed the *Bint al Hadash* in it. It was the only one of its kind in the container. Then we left the hut and sat on the straw mat. Fatouma soon became clearly troubled. "It's not right to put the wrong perfume in the baata. Let us go and inspect the container." We went back into the hut. She picked up the baata and slowly lifted its lid. The vial of *Bint al Hadash* I had purchased was broken into bits. "You see," she said, smiling, "the one above did not like this perfume. Go and buy some *Bint al Sudan.*"

I returned to the same shop and bought the right kind of perfume. Fatouma opened the perfume so I could learn its fragrance—very strong and sweet. She then closed it rapidly, entered her hut, and put the vial in the baata. We sat down once again on the straw mat and she took out her divining cowry shells—seven of them. "If the one who is above accepts your offering, you will smell the fragrance as it wafts from the hut over to us." As she began to throw the cowries and divine my future, we looked at one another. The sweet and strong fragrance of *Bint al Sudan* was in the air. She told me to breathe it in deeply. I did as she asked. The air around us was premeated with *Bint al Sudan*. I did not ask her how this could happen. I certainly did not know *why* this was happening. She threw the cowries once again and said: "It is time that you learn the secrets of reading cowries."

*   *   *

Two vignettes from the field. Two vignettes on the paradoxical nature of anthropological work. My first attempt to learn about the Songhay through a questionnaire was an unqualified failure; all of my respondents lied to me. Perhaps much of the blame was mine. Perhaps my questionnaire was not well-designed. Perhaps I abandoned too rapidly an epistemology in which the goal is to produce ideal, verifiable, and replicable knowledge that we might use as a data base for comparison. But my personal interest in religion and the imponderables of magic, witchcraft, and sorcery pushed me to choose a more subjective approach to fieldwork—letting the Songhay teach me about their culture and society.[1] This approach led me over the years to meet and know people, not informants; it led me inside a sorko's hut; it led me beyond an invisible threshold to a domain the Songhay call the "world of eternal war." In this "world of eternal war" much has happened that I have not been able to explain or understand. How could I explain, after all, the broken vial of *Bint al Hadash?* Sleight of hand, remembering so vividly Lévi-Strauss's "Sorcerer and his Magic"?[2] Perhaps the force of the spirit broke the vial? Maybe this woman, despite our budding relationship, was, for any number of reasons, trying to deceive me?

While I prefer to be led by others into murky worlds where I attempt to unravel the mysteries of metaphor, illusion, humor, or symbolism, this subjective approach is not foolproof. Even when an anthropologist has gained the confidence of people after ten, twenty, or thirty years, he or she may still be the victim of misinterpretation, innuendo, and deceit. I know of Songhay who continue their attempt to deceive Jean Rouch, even though he has been a sensitive, knowledgeable and respected participant in Songhay social life for more than forty years.

What are we to make of these fundamental problems? Are these cases representative of most anthropological work? If we transcend the limitations of the Western empirical tradition, whatever that may be, what remains? Are we left with a subjectivism so laced with imperfections that it, too, is worthless? Perhaps we should be more realistic about the goals of the human sciences and take the sober advice of David Hume, who wrote that "all our reasonings concerning causes and effects are derived from nothing but custom; and that belief is more properly an act of the sensitive, than the cogitative part of our nature."[3]

This chapter follows Hume's advice by assessing the sense of "anthropological science." Can we discover the Truth of Human Nature? Are there underlying Laws of Culture? Do we waste our time and resources through endless theorizing, as we try to discover the Ultimate and the Absolute in our search for the Truth?

Anthropology has one strength: ethnography, the original, albeit imperfect, product of our discipline. Despite its taken-for-granted status, ethnography, rather than cultural materialism, structuralism, or any other "ism," has been and will continue to be our core contribution. It is time to appreciate ethnographers who produce works of art that become powerful vehicles of theoretical exposition.[4]

PLATO: THE EPISTEME AND THE SCIENCE OF ANTHROPOLOGY

Much of Michel Foucault's work focused on the episteme, "that apparatus which makes possible the separation of not the true from the false, but of what may from what may not be characterized as scientific."[5] In his diverse works on madness, sexuality, criminal justice, medicine, and the history of the human sciences, Foucault demonstrated how the episteme governs what we see, what we think, what we say, and what we write. He also described how historical forces have combined in different periods of time to change a given episteme. He wrote of the episteme of the Renaissance, in which words had an existence of their own. He described the classical episteme, an age of *mathesis,* in which words were neutral, conveyors of pure representation in a mechanistic order. He discussed the modern episteme, in which scholars discovered the finitude of man, a discovery that heralded the human sciences. And yet the human sciences present, as Foucault suggested, an epistemological paradox:

> Not only are the human sciences able to do without a concept of man, they are unable to pass through it, for they always address themselves to that which constitutes his outer limits. One may say of them what Lévi-Strauss said of ethnology: that they dissolve man.[6]

Lévi-Strauss's comment may seem misguided, unless one considers the development of the scientific epistemology that Whitehead, among others, considered Plato's legacy. Foucault notwithstanding, the search for Truth transcends any episteme and dissolves human *being* in the human sciences.

The Legacy of Plato

Plato emerged in Greek thinking at a time of systematic reflection, creating order from chaos. Consider, for example, Heraclitus's attempt to characterize the perception of Being:

> Do not listen to me, the moral speaker, but be in hearkening to the Laying that gathers; first belong to this and then you hear properly; such hearing *is* when a letting-lie-together-before occurs by which the gathering letting-lie, the Laying that gathers, lies before us gathered; when a letting-lie-before occurs, the fateful comes to pass.[7]

From these philosophical fragments Plato devised the search for Truth, to paraphrase Richard Rorty, in which we turn away from subjectivity (Heraclitus's oblique writing) to objectivity. Objectivity was Plato's solution to the puzzle of infinite variability in the world of appearances. And so Plato was the first thinker to distinguish appearance from reality: behind every appearance there is a hidden, immutable Form. These Forms are the archetypes of knowledge, distinguished from opinion, which, in Plato's view, is as unstable as the flux of appearances. Knowledge, on the other hand, is an immutable pillar of reality.[8]

From these simple distinctions, the epistemology of Western philosophy was born. These metaphysical distinctions, I suggest, have not been disputed by others since Plato; rather, thinkers have disputed only how to discover the reality hidden behind appearances, how to arrive at Truth.

Saussure's Signs

Rousseau began an era in which scholars searched for Platonic Truth in the origins of things: the origin of society through an examination of pristine groups; the origin of language in comparative philology. Saussure, seeking the structure (reality) behind the variable surface of speech, argued for the synchronic study of language. In systematic linguistics, language (*langue*) contrasts with speech (*parole*). *Langue* "is not to be confused with human speech (*langage*), of which it is a definite part. It (*langue*) is both a social product of the faculty of speech and a collection of necessary conventions that have been adopted by a social body to permit individuals to exercise that faculty."[9] Saussure considered speech (*parole*) beyond his study, for it is so heterogeneous that "We cannot put it into any category of human facts, and we cannot discover its unity."[10] Saussure further emphasized the primacy of *langue* over *parole:* "Language [*langue*] . . . is a self-contained whole and a principle of classification. As soon as we give language [*langue*] first place among the facts of speech, we introduce natural order into a mass that lends itself to no other classification."[11] In seeking the ultimate Truth of language, Saussure, like Plato, sought the One, *langue,* in this case an elegantly self-contained whole, in the Many, *parole,* a heterogeneous tangle of variability.

Saussure also distinguished signifier from signified, and for him the sign consisted of "the whole that results from the associating of signifier to signified."[12] In its relationship of the signifier to the signified, the sign is an immutable form. Although time does change linguistic signs, the fundamental relationship between signifier and signified transcends the temporary; it remains unchanged. This is tantamount to saying that the relationship of signifier to signified is an immutable form, the One underlying the Many.

The work of Saussure set the stage for two major movements in social science: structural linguistics and structuralism. The structural linguists were inspired by Saussure's notion of synchrony, as well as by his idea that linguistics is the study of *langue* rather than *parole.* The Prague School of Linguistics took up structural analysis in phonology. In the United States, by contrast, Bloomfield extended the structural analysis of *langue* to morphology, syntax, and semantics. In both schools, units of analysis—phonemes, morphemes, syntagmemes, and so on—were all-important. For structural linguists the phoneme is a construct quite different from the phone, the sounds of which are infinitely variable. The phoneme, a minimal unit of sound that has distributive meaning, limits the infinite variability of phones. Immutable phonemes are isolated through contrastive analysis; they are units that linguists induce from phones, or, put another way, from fleeting appearances.

Lévi-Strauss's debt to structural linguistics, especially to Roman Jakobson, a Prague school linguist, is well known. The structural liniguists taught Lévi-Strauss that language is a system of systems. And just as language is a system of systems, so culture, in Lévi-Strauss's view, is a system of systems. In culture, as in language, there are hidden elementary structures, discoverable through scientific analysis, that link not only past with present, but also the Rousseaurian primitive with the modern. Following in the footsteps of Saussure, Lévi-Strauss devised a method, structuralism, in which the One, cognitive structures common to all human beings, could be delimited from the Many, individual structural relations.

In his monumental *The Elementary Structures of Kinship,* Lévi-Strauss focused on the institution of marriage. Marriage practices seem beyond explanation, as they are so alarmingly variable. But Lévi-Strauss demonstrated that what appears to be marriage is in reality the exchange of women:

> In the course of this work, we have seen the notion of exchange become complicated and diversified; it has constantly *appeared* to us in different forms. Sometimes exchange appears direct. . . . Sometimes it functions within a total system . . . and at others it instigates the formation of an unlimited number of special systems and short cycles unconnected among themselves. . . . Sometimes the exchange is explicit . . . and at other times it is implicit. . . . Sometimes the exchange is closed, while at other times it is open. . . . But no matter what form it takes, whether direct or indirect, general or special, immediate or deferred, explicit or implicit, closed or open, concrete or symbolic, it is exchange, always exchange, that emerges as the fundamental and common basis of *all* modalities of the institution of marriage.[13]

To discover the meaning of a given institution, like marriage, the analyst uncovers the reality obscured by the haze of appearances. Like his intellectual ancestors from Plato on, Lévi-Strauss seeks the One among the Many:

> The ultimate goal of the human sciences is not to constitute man, but to dissolve him. The critical importance of ethnology is that it represents the first step in a process which includes others. Ethnologic analysis tries to arrive at invariants beyond the empirical diversity of societies. . . . This initial enterprise opens the way for others . . . which are incumbent on the natural sciences: the reintegration of culture into nature and generally of life into the whole of its physico-chemical conditions. . . . One can understand, therefore, why I find in ethnology the principle of all research.[14]

Ethnology is not only Lévi-Strauss's principle for all research, but the basis of the metaphysics founded by Plato more than 2,500 years ago.

Anthropological Adages

What has been good for Lévi-Strauss has been good for most anthropologists. I do not suggest that all anthropologists are latent structuralists; rather, I argue that most anthropologists are members of the community of Western metaphysicians. We, like Lévi-Strauss, search for the One in the Many; we seek out the Platonic Truth, the reality lurking behind appearances.

Radcliffe-Brown did not hesitate to place anthropological science within metaphysics. In numerous articles he stedfastly suggested that anthropology, or what he called comparative sociology, was a branch of the natural sciences in which scholars would induce social structures to be compared. Through comparison, Radcliffe-Brown, argued, anthropologists arrive inductively at "laws of social statics" (what Lévi-Strauss referred to as "invariants").[15] Plato, of course, referred to these "laws" as Forms. Like Radcliffe-Brown, Malinowski thought that general propositions can be induced from a mass of data. One first collects ethnographic facts, Malinowski tells us, and then analyzes them to see what patterns unfold.

These metaphysical patterns are present in recent theoretical orientations in anthropology. The ethnography of communication provides an example. Hymes argues for describing society from the vantage of communication (speaking). He points, rightly, to the importance of describing cultural conceptions from the point of view of those who are being studied—the so-called "emic grid." From emic data, the ethnographer of communication classifies communicative acts, events, or situations within their cultural context. Hymes warns, however, that taxonomy is not an end in itself; the object is the painstaking recording of ethnographic diversity: "The work of taxonomy is a necessary part of progress toward models (structural and generative) of sociolinguistic description, formulation of universal sets of features and relations, and explanatory theories."[16] Joining the universalists of the Platonic heritage, Hymes adds: "In sum, just as a theory of grammar must have its universal terms, so must a theory of language use."[17] Indeed, without the universal terms natural scentists use, how can sociolinguists or social scientists compare data from highly diverse societies? How can they achieve theoretical wholes from the muddle of variable data?

The taken-for-granted Platonic distinctions, which weave themselves into so many theories, also appear in some contemporary theories of ethnography. The New Ethnography was an attempt to produce reliable and valid ethnographic accounts. From Goodenough onward, the new ethnographers, who later became ethnoscientists and ethnosemanticists, formulated ideational theories of culture. Folk taxonomies, componential analysis, cognitive maps and rules, all of which were induced from carefully collected data, were etic reflections of the cognitive processes of a variety of peoples. As with the ethnography of communication, this research moved away from taxonomy toward a universal observation language to aid the analyst in the search for that ever-elusive reality hidden behind the mirage of data.

Agar has been particularly sensitive to the need for an ethnographic language. In one recent article he and Hobbs, a computer scientist, call for a theory of ethnography. They write that "ethnography needs theoretical guidelines for the analysis of 'informal ethnographic interviews.'"[18] They propose "Artificial Intellegence Planning" as a way of building a universal vocabulary in ethnography to make ethnographic analysis more systematic. As Agar points out, "we desperately need a language to talk about ethnography in a general way."[19] Following the lead of Saussure's discussion of *parole*, and Lévi-Strauss's analysis of marriage, Agar suggests that ethnographies, even on the same people or topic, are so diverse that they are difficult to compare. Agar seeks to place the "embarrassing" dissimilarities of written ethnographic accounts into a more systematic framework that he calls "knowledge representation." Here again, an innovative anthropologist looks "beneath" the phenomenon, to paraphrase Merleau-Ponty, for general principles to account for diversity: the One, an ethnographic language, in the Many.

Straw Men, Epistemes, and Discourse

The great logicians taught that the construction of straw men in arguments weakens a person's contentions. My discourse on Saussure and Lévi-Strauss has been designed to demonstrate anthropology's taken-for-granted membership in the Platonic tradition.[20] Were I to stop here, I would be guilty not only of logical fallacy, but also of intellectual negativism. Heirs of the Platonic tradition, anthropologists are caught in institutional webs; they work within an episteme that affects the discourse, the written product of scholarship, that they produce. The search for Truth dissolves humankind. In contemporary anthropology, as a consequence, theorizing becomes serious business. Theoretical treatises—on ethnography, kinship, exchange, symbolism, cognition—are much more highly valued than vivid description. Published work in anthropology therefore assesses ethnographic data from a Marxist perspective, from a cognitive perspective, from a Freudian perspective, *ad nauseam*.

Taken-for-granted metaphysics, Jacques Derrida warns, makes scholars lose sight of what is *in* the world.[21] Merleau-Ponty and Langer suggest in different works that scientific methods, assumptions, and discourse obscure rather than illumine questions of life and consciousness.[22] Caught in the web of metaphysics, we posit post-Socratic universal theory as an alternative to pre-Socratic chaos. Caught in these metaphysical webs, we produce a discourse that is flat and neutral.

WRITING AND THE TEXT OF TEXTS

Flat, neutral, and "sludgy" writing is endemic in anthropological discourse. I find examples of it every time I pick up a journal. I read a line or two, a page or two, rub my eyes, and put the journal down. No wonder, when I consider some typical openings, which Tedlock, Said, and others, consider rhetorically significant.[23]

> *Example 1.* Ethnologists and archaeologists, in general, have expressed relatively little interest in the development of a unified ecological view of aboriginal life in the Great Plains.[24]

> *Example 2.* In anthropological theory, variations in the sexual division of labor have often been seen as causes of variations in residence patterns, marriage practices, beliefs about gender, socialization patterns, and many other aspects of human behavior and belief.[25]

> *Example 3.* Interest in the way a "native" sees his or her culture has a long history in American anthropology, going back to Franz Boas, Ruth Benedict, Robert Lowie, Ralph Linton, and many others active in the first half of the 20th century. This interest has continued with new theories and methods of description, classification, and analysis of cultural phenomena.[26]

> *Example 4.* Cultural understandings about ethnic identity typically entail beliefs about personality traits characteristic of particular categories of people or groups.[27]

> *Example 5.* Anthropology in the English-speaking Caribbean is marked by an analytical antinomy that reflects the great historical ambiguity of Carribean societies.[28]

> *Example 6.* Gilbert (1981) concludes that corporate cognatic descent groups exist in upper class Lima [Peru] society.[29]

> *Example 7.* This paper concerns the communication of affect, and the role therein of cultural and linguistic systems. It explores some analytical issues in cross-cultural comparison and the notion of "expressive language" and it examines modes of affective expression in a particular ethnographic case.[30]

> *Example 8.* Kennan (1973:49) has defined the pragmatic presupposition as the "relation between the utterance of a sentence and the context in which it is uttered."[31]

This prose, including my own, reflects the alienation of the anthropological episteme. "The anthropologist who treats the indigene as an object may define himself as relatively free, but that is an illusion. For in order to objectify the other, one is, at the same time, compelled to objectify the self."[32] This objectification is expressed in anthropological discourse.

Monographs are not exempt from flat, neutral and sludgy writing, although, given the breadth of this form, there is opportunity for eye-opening, invigorating prose. But before a reader gets to the good stuff of a monograph—if there is any to be found—he or she suffers prefaces and introductions, which tend to be longer versions of the opening lines of journal articles. There are many exceptions, of course, but in prefaces or introductions, contemporary authors discuss their subject and their approach via a general review of the literature. Then the data are presented to underscore the major thesis of the book. Finally, the author summarizes the data and presents the conclusions.

How many recent monographs have begun like Raymond Firth's classic, *We, The Tikopia*, quoted in Chapter 2?[33] Firth's description is the stuff of classic ethnography, in which the anthropologist-as-writer considers the reader-as-reader, interpreting silently a book's multilogued prose. While one may view the ideas that seep out between the lines of *We, The Tikiopia* as dated, the prose of this magnificent ethnography leaves a vivid impression of the people of that island. Firth's detailed ethnography—imperfect, as are all ethnographies—became part of the ethnographic record, an eternal document in the history of humanity.

There are more recent examples of splendidly written ethnographies. One thinks of Michael Lambek's *Human Spirits*, with an introduction called "Cultural Zero," in which he describes his first encounter with spirit possession on the island of Mayotte.[34] There is John M. Chernoff's penetrating account of the sociocultural significance of drumming in Ghana.[35] There is Vincent Crapanzano's rich description of a Hamshida possession ritual in Morocco,[36] as well as his more recent work in South Africa.[37] And there is Jeanne Favret-Saada's highly personalized *Deadly Words:*

> Take an ethnographer; she has chosen to investigate contemporary witchcraft in the Bocage of Western France. She has already done some fieldwork; she has a basic academic training; she has published some papers on the logic of murder, violence, and insurrection in an altogether different tribal society. She is now working in France to avoid having to learn yet another difficult language. . . .
>
> Take an ethnographer. She has spent more than 30 months in the Bocage in Mayenne, studying witchcraft. "How exciting, how thrilling, how extraordinary . . . !" "Tell us about witches," she is asked again and again when she gets back to the city. Just as one might say: tell us about ogres and wolves, about Little Red Riding Hood. Frighten us, but make it clear that it's only a story; or that they are just peasants: credulous, backward, and marginal.[38]

This kind of lush, vivid, lyrical, and personal writing lies beyond the usual parameters of appropriateness that have been established within the episteme of anthropology. Unfortunately, one does not become a distinguished anthropologist because of the quality of one's prose or the memorability of one's descriptions.

Anthropological discourse is characterized by the search for "invariants beyond the empirical diversity of societies."[39] The search must isolate and account for aspects of human behavior, and not the murkiness and imprecision of human existence. In a recent article on "Human Linguistics," Ross skillfully highlights the relationship between episteme and discourse. Some linguists, he writes, are concerned with answering the question: "What formal principles, both language-particular and universal, are necessary and sufficient to characterize the distribution of and relationship among linguistic elements in each of the languages of the world?"[40] Human linguistics is concerned with an altogether different question: "What can the study of language tell us about human beings?"[41]

Plato, Art, and Metaphysics

The birth of metaphysics, of Ultimate Forms, of the search for Truth, set the boundaries between art and metaphysics. Plato wanted the dramatic artists expelled from his Republic, for the sentiments that dramatists are capable of provoking lead people back to the heroic myths and ignorance, rather than toward the discovery of Ultimate Forms. Plato, quoting Socrates, wrote:

> When any one of these pantomimic gentlemen, who are so clever that they imitate anything, comes to us, and makes a proposal to exhibit himself and his poetry, we will fall down and worship him as a sweet and holy and wonderful being, but we must also inform him that in our State such as he are not permitted to exist; the law will not allow them.[42]

And why not? Because in the State, the poet or dramatist does not fit into any of the social categories prescribed by the doctrine of Ultimate Forms. Put another way, art and metaphysics become mutually exclusive; hence the presence of flat, neutral, and sludgy prefaces, pretexts, and texts in the discourse of the human sciences.

Yet, when anthropologists are confronted with something they cannot explain, they find that the foundation of this aged metaphysics begins to crumble, that the discourse that worked so well in a previous study cannot adequately represent a particular field incident.

Art and science should complement one another. Indeed, if we focus on anthropological texts not as explicit logico-deductive/inductive statements, but rather as texts that describe the texture of a society to a reader, the possibility of this complementarity stares us in the face. Merleau-Ponty called on philosophers to use language to bring readers into contact with "brute and wild being" (see Chapter 2).[43] Anthropologists, too, need to confront language in its full being and not as a neutral mechanism of representation. Consider the words of Heidegger:

> To undergo an experience with language, then, means to let ourselves be properly concerned by the claim of language by entering into and submitting to it. If it is true that man finds the proper abode of his existence in language—whether he is aware of it or not—then an experience we undergo with language will touch the innermost nexus of our existence. We who speak language may thereupon become transformed by such experiences, from one day to the next or in the course of time. But now it could be that an experience we undergo with language is too much for us moderns, even if it strikes us only to the extent that for once it draws our attention to our *relation to language,* so that from then on we may keep this relation in mind.[44]

Ross seems to have experienced the Being of language; his article, "Human Linguistics" is a poem that is a multilogue. It not only concerns a current debate in theoretical linguistics, but also suggests a fundamental shift toward humanism in the most positivistic of the social sciences. Favret-Saada and Contreras wrote an ethnography in the literary form of a diary, where they record Favret-Saada's experience in the Bocage of western France. This diary becomes an open window through which the reader is swept into the Bocage. Readers experience the authors' joy, doubts, fears, and disappointments.[45]

THE RECONSTRUCTION OF ETHNOGRAPHY

Even if one has experienced the Being of language, one is still caught in the straitjacket of the episteme, anthropological or otherwise. One cannot perceive, conceive, speak, or write in a cultural vacuum. My discourse in this chapter has followed a standard form (introduction, review of the pertinent literature, argument, and conclusion). We anthropologists are all caught in an epistemological double bind: we seek Truth, the One in the Many; we covet abstract principles as we distinguish opinion from knowledge; we create categories of appearance and reality; we posit domains of metaphysics (or science) and of art; we create one discourse for metaphysics and one for art. And even if we transcend the limitations posed by all these binary oppositions—to blend science with art—our categories, as Hume wrote, are still derived from custom.[46]

What remains in this philosophical rubble? Perhaps I can say that anthropologists can never be engineers; we must remain *bricoleurs* rummaging through the debris of deconstructed ideas for something new and meaningful. But that something new for which we search endlessly has but one fate: to be deconstructed in its own turn. For Derrida, "knowledge is not a systematic tracking down of truth that is hidden but may be found. It is rather the field of '*free play,*' that is to say, a field of infinite substitutions in the closure of a finite ensemble.' "[47] Derrida's critique of Western philosophy offers no alternative to a world without metaphysical foundation. Must we go to these Derridean extremes? I think not. Realistically, an anthropology formulated on positivistic or phenomenological grounds is full of imperfections. But from the debris of these imperfections, I suggest the possibility of a reconstruction of ethnography.

This reconstruction would not concern a theory to discuss ethnography in a general way.[48] Indeed, a theory of ethnography would only make anthropology more like a "real science," to allow us to avoid the "embarrassment" of not having a theory of something—ethnography—which "is at the heart of anthropologies that deal with living peoples."[49] The reconstruction of ethnography is rather a call for a humanistic anthropology, a call for meaningful descriptions of what Armstrong called "human being," a call for fine ethnographies like Fernandez's *Bwiti* and Rose's *Black American Street Life.*[50]

The reconstruction of ethnography, however, implies a great deal more than a valorization of ethnographic writing; it implies a fundamental epistemological shift toward Others and away from ethnographic realism. We need to describe others as people and give them a voice in our discourse. We need to write ethnographies as multilayered texts that communicate to a number of audiences. We need to acknowledge in the text the presence of an ethnographer who engages in dialogue with his or her subjects.

*   *   *

I returned to Mehanna in 1982–83 to continue my studies of the Songhay. One morning as I trudged along the paths that cut through the walled compounds of the town, I greeted Amadu, a bent-over old man well into his seventies. For more than five years, I had greeted this man as I walked by his compound. "How is your wife?" "How are your wife's people?" "How are the people of your compound?" "How is your health?" He would always respond that all was well and would ask after my health. Until that day in 1983 I knew nothing else about this man.

"I am glad to learn you are in good health, my son," he said to me that morning. (Songhay elders often call younger men, "my son.")

"That I am, Baba [father]."

"For five years you have greeted me."

"That is true."

"And you have asked nothing of me?"

"True."

"For five years I have watched you, and today you shall know me. Come into my house. I like you and this is why I shall give you the story of me life."

I wondered what he would tell me. Inside his dark thatched hut was an altar. Miniature leather sandals and small clay jugs tied to pieces of cloth hung from bundles of sticks that formed the skeleton of the hut.

"I am a zima, and I have been one for more than fifty years."

"I did not know, Baba."

"We Songhay do not talk of our strengths to anyone. We must know people first. I know you now, my son, and I want you to know me. Go and get your machine [tape recorder] so you can open it and learn my story."

I went to get my tape recorder and "opened" it for this warm, wise man. An orphan, he left the island of his birth, Sinder, as a young man. He traveled about the Sahel in search of work, mostly as a farmhand. He then traveled to Aribinda, the great center of farming magic in Burkina Faso, where he apprenticed himself to a master sorcerer. After seven years in Aribinda, he traveled to the Borgu in northern Togo, where he again apprenticed himself to a master sorcerer. Seven years later he returned to Niger and spent one year in Sangara, one of the magic villages of Songhay. There he learned about the Songhay spirits and became a zima. After fifteen years of training he settled in Mehanna, where he became the priest of the local possession troupe. By the time I met him, Amadu Zima's body was bowed with age—like the dessicated trunk of a giant acacia dying ever so slowly. He had long since given up being a zima, but clients still sought his services—for sorcery. He never left his compound.

After recounting in detail the history of his life, Amadu Zima discussed with me Songhay philosophy and sorcery. He spoke about the spirits, recited incantations and praise-poetry, revealed the secret names of medicinal plants, and performed three rites that would protect me from the vicissitudes of enemies and spirits alike.

We talked for weeks, and throughout our discussions Amadu Zima continued to proclaim how much he liked me. "I would never tell this to anyone," he said. "But I tell my life, my secrets, to you, Paul, because I like you. You like me. You ask questions. You want to learn my ways. You are like the son I never had."

Amadu Zima does not represent all the Songhay; his story is his own. Yet how can we ignore such a man in the name of ethnographic realism? How can we ignore what the Amadu Zimas and Fatouma Seynis teach us about ourselves, about life? Is it not their voices that will help us to reconstruct ethnography?

9 | Detours

We shall not cease from exploration.
And the end of all our exploring
Will be to arrive where we started
And know the place for the first time.

T. S. Eliot

In the actual use of expressions we make detours, we go by sideroads. We see the straight highway before us, but of course we cannot use it, because it is permanently closed.

Wittgenstein

In language and life, human beings are meanderers; we continually take detours. Artists, philosophers and ethnographers often take sideroads which lead them into dimensions of time-space that stray far from the main highway. But too many of us describe those sideroads *as if* they were still the main highway. The result is a "straight" discourse—sometimes analogic, sometimes digital—suggesting that we have taken highways that lead us directly to our theoretical destinations, suggesting that we "know the place for the first time."

This straight discourse permeates the social sciences. We use it to write research proposals. Imagine a proposal in which the all-important methodology sections listed a series of improvisations—Hey, I'll just follow my intuitions—rather than a carefully prepared research design. We use straight discourse to write most of our articles and books, which consistently present in the timeless present scientific results in the prescribed

Figure 14: Sohanci Adamu Jenitongo, master of "detours"

forms I discussed in the prior chapter. Imagine articles and books which
dwell upon the sideroads of discovery rather than the main highway of
results.

It would be foolish to suggest that the "conventions of representation"
in the social sciences completely exclude surrealist methodologies and
epistemological essays.[1] They don't. Michel Leiris's magnificent *Afrique
fantôme,* his journal of the famous Dakar-Djibouti Mission (1931–33) is a

product of automatic writing.[2] In *Deadly Words* Jeanne Favret-Saada uses the subject of witchcraft in France to explore the epistemology of the social sciences.[3] And yet these works do not conform to the representational conventions of contemporary social science.[4]

The question of human meandering makes ethnographers uncomfortable, for it once again forces us to confront some of the more embarrassing debates in anthropological history—Redfield vs. Lewis; Freeman vs. Mead. These were cases in which anthropological studies of the same village (Redfield and Lewis in Mexico) or the same society (Mead and Freeman in Samoa) produced drastically different results. Does this mean that Redfield and Mead were correct and Lewis and Freeman wrong in their assessments of Mexican villages and Samoan society? Are scholars ever correct or accurate in the human sciences? Can we extract from ethnographic data first principles, laws, axioms, theorems? What do we see in the worlds of others? Some of us see rules; others see theoretical refinements of Marxism, structuralism, functionalism. Scholars also see systems—social, ethnomedical, ethnosemantic, or otherwise. We all see "society" and "culture," the elusive terms we created to make sense of other worlds. In exploding the myth of conversational "rules," the late Erving Goffman put the matter of what there *is* in a clear perspective:

> An adjacent hearer can elect to let the matter entirely pass, tacitly framing it as though it were the stomach rumblings of another's mind, and continue on undeflected from his task involvements; or, for example, he can hit upon the venting as an occasion to bring the remaining company into a focus of conversation attention for a jibe made at the expense of another person who introduced the initial distraction, which efforts these others may decline to support, and if declining, provide no display of excuse for doing so. In these circumstances the whole framework of conversational constraints—both system and ritual—can become something to honor, to invert, or to disregard, depending as the mood strikes. On these occasions it's not merely that the lid can't be closed; there is no box.[5]

And if this kind of "free play" pops out of illusionary conversational boxes, what can be said of the mind-boggling "free play" that explodes from the illusionary boxes of society and culture?

How does the ethnographer apprehend the elusiveness of worlds in which he or she tries to close the lid to discover that there is no box? Keats long ago had an answer in his concept of "negative capability." Dewey notes that, for Keats, Shakespeare was a man of enormous "negative capability," the capacity of "being in uncertainties, mysteries, doubts, without any irritable reaching after fact or reason."[6] Keats contrasted Shakespeare with Coleridge, who lacked the great playwright's "negative capability." Coleridge would "let a poetic insight go when it was surrounded with obscurity, because he could not intellectually justify it; could not, in Keats's language, be satisfied with '*half*–knowledge.' "[7] In worlds rife with ambiguities, indeterminacies, and obscurities, "reason at its height cannot attain complete grasp and self-contained assurance. It must fall back upon imagination—upon the embodiment of ideas in emotionally charged sense."[8]

In this chapter I suggest that *detours* are paths that lead us to the realm of "negative capability," paths that ethnographers clearly need to take to set themselves straight with the world as it is. To demonstrate the ethnographic applicability of detours, of "negative capability," I shall discuss the self-acknowledged detours taken by a philosopher, Richard Rorty, and an artist, the late Joseph Beuys. Both of these men traveled the secondary roads of inner space and have concluded that scholars and artists can no longer nestle within the comfortable confines of their Truth-seeking disciplinary institutions; rather scholars must extend themselves to others in order to initiate and maintain a dialogue—to keep the conversation going, to heal imbalances between the "savage" and the "civilized," the natural and the mechanistic. Discussion of these philosophic and artistic detours sets the stage for an excursion into the pragmatist notion of radical empiricism—a detour leading, perhaps, to a more sensual, open ethnography.

PHILOSOPHICAL DETOURS: RICHARD RORTY

Richard Rorty was trained in analytic philosophy, the aim of which has been to discover a universal objective language, a truthful language that constitutes an objective reality. But in his monumental book, *Philosophy and the Mirror of Nature*, he describes his long intellectual journey from a philosophy that mirrors "Man's Glassy Essence" to a philosophy without mirrors in which human beings stand in relation to one another in the clasp of group solidarity. Rorty's book, to return to Wittgenstein, is the story of his acknowledged detour-taking. By following various tracks, Rorty traveled from systematic philosophy to an edifying philosophy, the major goal of which is not to uncover the Truth, but to maintain the conversation of humankind.

Philosophy With Mirrors

Since Plato, the great thrust of philosophical work has been in the area of systematic contemplation, the major thoroughfare of philosophy. The constructivists from Plato and Aristotle to Descartes and Leibniz have all been concerned with the relationship of human beings to a nonhuman reality—to an objective reality. From classical times through the Enlightenment to today, the philosopher has sought to distance himself "from the actual persons around him not by thinking of himself as a member of some other real or imaginary group, but rather by attaching himself to something which cannot be described with reference to any particular human beings."[9]

Plato was the master mirror-maker. From the philosophical fragments of the pre-Socratics he devised the notion of the search for Truth, in which we turn away from subjective involvement to objectivity. As we have seen in Chapter 7, Plato's quest for Truth (or Forms) through objectivity was his solution to the puzzle of the infinite variability found in the world of appearances. For Plato, knowledge becomes an immutable pillar of reality. Arising from Plato's foundation, "the picture that holds traditional philosophy captive is that of the mind as a great mirror, containing various representations—some accurate, some not—and capable of being studied by pure, nonempirical methods."[10] From this conception of mind there is derived the notion of "Our Glassy Essence":

> Our Glassy Essence was not a philosophical doctrine, but a picture which literate men found presupposed by every page they read. It is glassy—mirror like—for two reasons. First, it takes on new forms without being changed—but intellectual forms, rather than sensible ones as material mirrors do. Second, mirrors are made of a substance that is purer, finer grained, more subtle, and more delicate than most. Unlike our spleen, which, in combination with other equally gross and visible organs, accounted for the bulk of our behavior, our Glassy Essence is something we share with the angels, even though they weep for our ignorance of its essence. The supernatural world, for the sixteenth century intellectuals, was modeled upon Plato's world of Ideas, just as our contact with it was modeled upon his metaphor of vision.[11]

In short, Our Glassy Essence—the mind as mirror—is that which separates human from animal, civilized from savage; it is a creator of metaphoric guardrails along the philosophical highway.

In the development of systematic philosophy, a philosophy with which Rorty and all professional philosophers have been affiliated, the boundaries between appearance and reality, mind and body, self and society, civilized and savage, nature and culture, idealism and materialism—all of these—become reified. They become reflections of Our Glassy Essence. Accordingly, Rorty writes of his grand tour on the sideroads of behaviorism, skepticism, materialism, epistemology and the philosophy of mind, epistemology and empirical psychology, epistemology and the philosophy of language, and epistemology and hermeneutics. On each sideroad, he describes in lucid prose the logical potholes of say, behaviorism, materialism, or epistemology and the philosophy of mind. He demonstrates—at times quite brilliantly—the philosopher's desperate search for frameworks that would allow for the Truth of propositions, to uncover the One in the Many. More relevant to discourse today, philosophy "has made it its business to present a permanent neutral framework for culture. This framework is built around a distinction between inquiry into the real—the disciplines which are on the 'secure path of a science'—and the rest of culture."[12]

This philosophical framework may be fine for those engaged in the natural sciences, but it is limiting for many scholars in the human sciences who struggled to make the study of humanity an inquiry into the real, a veritable science. As indicated in Chapter 8, Lévi-Strauss's structuralism is an extreme expression of this tendency.

Scientism, in fact, reigns in the human sciences because we continue to believe the mind to be a pure mirror and that Our Glassy Essence enables us to find the One in the Many, the irreducible invariants beneath the surface diversity of appearances. In this tradition scholars search for simple sociobiological explanations of human behavior, and for theories of ethnography.[13] The search for universal Truth in the hard sciences, social sciences, and philosophy is business-as-usual; it is philosophy with mirrors.

Philosophy Without Mirrors

Rorty suggests that so long as philosophers believe in essences—that the world is constituted by clearly bounded and knowable things—philosophy will continue to be a search for immutable knowledge, the search for Truth. Since the latter part of the nineteenth century, however, a few wandering wayfarers have been bold enough to challenge the absolutist visions of knowledge and truth. "Truth lives, in fact," William James wrote, "for the most part on a credit system. Our thoughts and beliefs 'pass,' so long as nothing challenges them, just as bank notes pass so long as nobody refuses them."[14] My quoting James is not to assert that objective truth is impossible, but to point to the complementary notion of edification. Rorty says there are those philosophers who construct systems of knowledge; they ramble on the roadway of Western metaphysics, the descendants of Plato and Aristotle. On the access roads are those philosophers who write to edify, to educate, to keep the conversation going in the community of scholars. "For Heidegger, Sartre, and Gadamer, objective inquiry is perfectly possible and frequently actual—the only thing to be said against it is that it provides only some, among many, ways of describing ourselves, and that some of these can hinder the process of edification."[15]

A philosophy without mirrors, then, is a suggestive and educative philosophy. It is also a kind of pragmatic philosophy that seeks practical solidarity in a living community rather than rarefied objectivity in a mechanistic system. Rorty compares systematic philosophy (with mirrors) to edifying philosophy (without mirrors).

> Great constructive philosophers are constructive and offer arguments. Great edifying philosophers are reactive and offer satires, paraodies, aphorisms. They know their work loses its point when the period they were reacting to is over.

They are intentionally peripheral. Great systematic philosophers, like great scientists, build for eternity. Great edifying philosophers destroy for the sake of their own generation. Systematic philosophers want to put their subject on the secure path of science. Edifying philosophers want to keep space open for the sense of wonder which poets can sometimes cause—wonder that there is something new under the sun which is *not* an accurate representation of what was already there, something which (at least for the moment) cannot be explained and can barely be described.[16]

Truth, indeed, lives on a credit system. And so Rorty leaves us a fleeting sense of truth; his series of detours have led us to a bleak place where conversation has replaced Truth, where practical solidarity (filiation) has replaced absolute objectivity (affiliation).[17] Rorty's arguments weaken considerably the 2500-year tradition of Western metaphysics. But has Rorty taken us on so many detours that we have gone beyond the fringe?

ARTISTIC DETOURS: JOSEPH BEUYS

The late Joseph Beuys is known as the founder of the performance art movement. As an outgrowth of his early work in sculpture, he staged Happenings, multimedia events that challenged the artificial boundaries—disciplinary boundaries—that have been established in the humanities and the sciences. Like Rorty, Beuys took many detours, all of which were acknowledged in his art, to reach the destination of the Happening, or what Beuys called "Actions."

During World War II Beuys was a pilot in the German Air Force. During one mission over Russia in the dead of winter he was shot down over Crimea. The Tartars who discovered him wrapped him in felt and fur, keeping him warm and alive. After the war, Beuys became an artist who transformed concretely elements of his personal past into his artistic expression; fur and felt—which saved his life in the Crimea—became the major materials of his sculpture. Although many art historians write of Beuys as a sculptor, it would be a mistake to classify his work as "sculpture" or "kinetic art" or anything else, for the message in his work is that there are no discrete boundaries in a world that is in continuous flux; there are only ongoing processes. And so Beuys's Actions involved elements of sculpture, theater, poetry, philosophy, and expository discourse—all elements of a Happening, the purpose of which is to challenge the major themes of Western epistemology.

Of Beuys's many Actions, one of the best known was called *How to Explain Pictures to a Dead Hare*. In this Action, Beuys covered his head with gold leaf and honey and tied an iron sole to his right foot and a felt sole to his left foot. Meanwhile, he cradled a dead hare in his arms.

The image of the artist anointed, silently mouthing to a mute animal what cannot be said to his fellow man, became one of the most resonant images of the

1960s. But beyond that the appeal of *How to Explain Pictures to a Dead Hare* lies in the combination of that title, which says much about our anxious need for explanations, with the ritual mask through which the identity of man is psychologically obscured, and the intimate inclusion, where we are excluded, of an animal in a total state of vulnerability.[18]

Veering off the artistic path, Beuys was eager to discuss the whys and wherefores of his art, for his expository discourse was an essential aspect of his work. Symbolically, Beuys linked the hare to women, birth, and menstruation, and he suggested the hare incarnates himself into the earth. The hare rubs, pushes, and digs itself into the earth and enters its law; human beings, by contrast, are fundamentally mental creatures who incarnate themselves in the earth through thought. The honey coating Beuys's head referred to thinking. Human beings do not produce honey; they produce ideas. When Beuys put honey on his head he infused life into non-animate thinking.

Gold and honey indicate a transformation of the head, and therefore naturally and logically, the brain and our understanding of thought, consciousness and all the other levels necessary to explain pictures to a hare: the warm stool insulated with felt, the "radio" made of bone and electrical components under the stool and the iron sole with the magnet. I had to walk on this sole when I carried the hare round from picture to picture, so along with a strange limp came the clank of iron on the hard stone floor—that was all that broke the silence, since my explanations were mute, and the radio was on an almost inaudible wavelength.

This seems to have been the action that most captured people's imaginations. On one level this must be because everyone consciously or unconsciously recognizes the problem of explaining things, particularly where art and creative work are concerned, or anything that involves a certain mystery or questioning. The idea of explaining to an animal conveys a sense of secrecy of the world and of existence that appeals to the imagination. Then, as I have said, even a dead animal preserves more powers of intuition than some human beings with their stubborn rationality.[19]

Beuys believed that understanding is multileveled, encompassing imagination, intuition as well as rational thought. For Beuys, then, art became a form of sensual epistemological criticism.

Social Sculpture

Once one has become sensitive to Beuys's frameworks, the melange of forms that comprise his Actions, then he or she can apprehend the social significance of this sculpture. Beuys's theory of social sculpture is best exemplified in his work, *Fat Corner*. In *Fat Corner*, fat, generally margarine, is wedged into a corner of a room in the form of an equilateral triangle. There it is left to decompose. Eventually the fat is absorbed by the walls and the floor of the room; it has been transformed from a solid form with extrinsic order to a liquid form without order.

Some scholars have suggested that the fat in *Fat Corner* is the best substance to demonstrate Bueys's theory of sculpture. At warm temperatures, fat is a malleable solid that can be molded into desired shapes; it is an ordered solid. Fat is therefore "a paradox when it is placed in that most ordered of forms, a right-angled corner or wedge."[20] In Western society the corner symbolizes our space: buildings, rooms, city plans. The right angle is the cornerstone of our orientation to space. Indeed, the right angle reaches the limit of the continuum, Chaotic-Ordered. Just as the shaman manipulates a combination of symbols to bring about healthful social harmony, so Beuys's juxtaposition of diverse elements in *Fat Corner* demonstrates the link of the chaotic to the ordered in a world without myths and boundaries.

> Ideally a balance should be achieved, though the overriding tendency today is towards the intellectual pole. Balance, reintegration and flexible flow between the areas of thinking, feeling and will, all of which are essential, are the objective of the Theory. The moulding processes of art are taken as a metaphor of society; hence SOCIAL SCULPTURE.[21]

SHAMANISM IN ART AND PHILOSOPHY

In his various Actions, Joseph Beuys took the role of the shaman, a person who attempts to cure illness through rites that are designed to restore social balance. Through shamanistic performance the artist acts out his or her art. In most artistic circles it is considered appropriate to let a piece of sculpture, a painting, or a poem stand for itself. Why act it out? Why did Beuys place his sculpture in a dramatic context?

Some critics suggest that individualized drama constitutes the significant expressive form in the contemporary world.

> as our mythic structure deteriorates, the archetypes vanish and it is the trials and psychodramas of the individual that provide us with our sense of direction. . . . At this most crucial and sensitive point the artist focuses upon the minimal aspects of his own creative motivation.[22]

At first glance one would expect that these individualized dramas are grossly narcissistic; Beuys, after all, was the central character in all of his Actions.

In the contemporary world, however, there is emerging a new definition of self in aesthetic domains; it is an opaque self, the catalyst for expression. Along the route of performance art-theater, Beuys presented his Actions in what Barthes called "the middle voice."

> the middle voice corresponds exactly to the state of the verb to write: today to write is to make oneself the center of the action of speech [*parole*]; it is to effect

> writing in being affected oneself; it is to leave the writer [*scripteur*] inside the
> writing, not as a psychological subject . . . but as an agent of the action.[23]

Like certain modern writers who let language speak for itself, Beuys used himself as a tool to let his Actions express themselves. He became a modern ritual specialist—an artistic shaman. "Beuys' exercise of the shaman's position, operating in the middle voice, provides a frame within which philosophy may be rethought."[24]

Just as Beuys's shamanistic performances in the middle voice provide a new detour for art, so Rorty's new pragmatism yields new directions for philosophical inquiry. Both men fit the category of edification. The purpose of art-philosophy for them is to educate, to restore balance (Beuys) and solidarity (Rorty) in a human community. The work of both men seeks to heal the world of its most pernicious malady: the totalizing terror the absolutism of which threatens to destroy humankind. They say we need to keep our conversations going; they show that we need to feel the threads that connect the chaotic to the ordered.

ANTHROPOLOGICAL DETOURS: RADICAL EMPIRICISM

Most anthropologists today walk a liminal path that meanders through the sciences and humanities. Are we real social scientists who seek to discover the invariate truths of social existence? Or, are we real storytellers who seek to recreate for our readers the texture of social life in other societies. Or, as one young anthropologist put it recently, is the ongoing debate about the putative scientific nature of anthropology depressingly boring?

Such questions have been asked for centuries. In classical times, Plato wanted Greek storytellers (poets and dramatists) expelled from his Republic. But Sextus Empiricus, the principal Pyrrhonian skeptic, deplored Plato's philosophy and warned the Greeks of the evils of the latter's "dogmatism."[25] Over time the influence of Plato's mainstream "dogmatism" far outdistanced the impact of Sextus's minority tradition of skepticism. The classical humanism of Kant and Hegel built on Platonic foundations the philosophical edifices that became the Enlightenment, a body of ideas in which intellectualism, the power of pure thought, reigns over such other human faculties as feeling and action (see Chapters 1 and 2). Such a pervasive body of ideas left little room for the storytellers, who were still excluded from Reason's castle.

Early in the twentieth century the storytellers, a motley assortment of artists and dramatists, experimented with reality. They transformed dreams into tableaux and effects into causes. Their artistic movements (futurism, cubism, dadaism, surrealism) savaged the reigning intellectualism of their time through the imagery of objects and words arranged in new, disquieting ways.[26] They were like the Greek skeptics in a way: they offered no detailed alternatives to intellectualism. The storytellers preferred to point to the dangers of contemporary "dogmatism," and to the liberating effects of piercing through the world's superficialities. While high "modernism" rocked the world of the arts, it had little impact on the sciences, human or otherwise.

But the tradition of skepticism did not die with high modernism. In the past twenty years a new skepticism has appeared on the intellectual horizon. Such writers as Foucault, Derrida, and Lyotard have further exposed the failures of intellectualism, suggesting that it has not brought us freedom from ignorance—as promised by the likes of Socrates, Plato, Kant, and Hegel; rather, it has brought us terror and totalitarianism.[27] The impact of Derridean "free play" or Lyotardian "gaming" has eroded as never before the solid foundation of Reason. The certainty, determinism, and clarity of classical humanism have been replaced by the uncertainty, indeterminacy, and ambiguity of the contemporary age. "Human scientists" have meandered onto the detour of Keats's aforementioned "negative capability."

According to John Dewey, two major premises emerge from Keats's ideas on "negative capability." The first is that the origin of reasonings has a spontaneous "instinctive" quality which makes reasonings immediate, sensuous, and poetic. The second is that "no 'reasoning' as reasoning, that is, excluding imagination and sense, can reach truth."[28]

Experience, of course, is what Keats's "negative capability" is all about. As Dewey strongly suggested, experience is a radically empirical domain in which thoughts, feelings, and actions are inseparable. Experience is continuous for every human being; it is not only ethereal, but fundamentally aesthetic. For Dewey, the aesthetic, an intrinsic component of experience, "is no intruder in experience from without, whether by way of idle luxury or transcendent ideality, but . . . it is the clarified and intensified development of traits that belong to every normally complete experience."[29] For Dewey, then, there is no intellectualist separation of ideal expression, Art, from prosaic expression, art or folk art. Art is part of experience and experience is part of art. There can be no idealization of experience, aesthetic or otherwise. In the tradition of Shakespeare, Montaigne, Keats, Nietzsche, Dewey, James, Foucault, Derrida, Rorty, and Beuys—skeptics all—the notion of truth "never signifies correctness of intellectual statements about things or truth as its meaning is influenced by science. It denotes the wisdom by which men live."[30] The aesthetic awareness of the senses, then, plays a foundational role in experience, which, in turn, is the heart of ethnographic fieldwork.

Radical Empiricism in Anthropology

Anthropologists have not turned a deaf ear to the emergent skepticism of deconstructionist theory and Rortian neo-pragmatism. Books and articles

by a growing number of scholars have focused on the theoretical implications of a changing world in which the indeterminate undermines our
"quest for certainty."[31] Although most of the authors of these works probe
the politics of representation—disciplinary, intercultural, or international—they generally fail to consider concretely how the shift toward the
indeterminate will affect anthropological writing.

In previous chapters I have focused on how our intellectual heritage—
a veritable escape from the senses—has affected the way we see, feel, smell,
hear, think, and write. We shall now focus even more concretely on how
taking the exit marked "Radical Empiricism" will contribute to the re-
generation of ethnography.

By now most of us know that culture, society, fieldwork are all contingent, ever-changing, slippery concepts. By now most of us admit that
social theory has failed to predict human behavior reliably and validly.[32]
What is left, then, in a world so filled with uncertainties? For a few anthropologists, these uncertainties are liberating; they allow us the latitude to
play with established disciplinary and literary conventions. In a radically
empirical ethnography devoid of intellectualist presuppositions, the unseen interpenetrates with the seen, the audible fuses with the tactile, and
the boundaries of literary genres are blurred. Elements of life history and
autobiography may be molded into an expository (realist) text. Confessions
may be problem-oriented. Ethnographic prose may take on a more literary
character with deep characterizations, vivid descriptions of place, sound,
smells, tastes, dialogue, plot, and drama. By taking a radically empirical
detour, anthropologists enter the sensual world of evocation, which, for us,
entails two forms of expression: film and narrative ethnography.

Ethnographic Film

Film can be a powerfully evocative medium, projecting to an audience a
narrative which may be infused with sensual sights and sounds. But sensual sights and sounds do not carry the burden of a film: that is the job of
the narrative, which, if constructed with care and creativity, can be moving.

The master of evocative ethnographic film is unquestionably the
French filmmaker and anthropologist Jean Rouch. Rouch's films of the
Songhay and Dogon peoples do not analyze the social phenomena that they
portray. Rather, they present imagery of such unforgettable power, as in
the possession scenes of the classic, *Les Maîtres fous*, that the viewer is
affected. Some viewers are repelled by the brutality of the Hauka spirits
who chomp on the boiled meat of a freshly slaughtered dog. Others are
awed by the power of these spirits who put their bare hands into boiling
cauldrons without ill effect. The images also compel most viewers to respect Songhay and Dogon living in their own worlds. Rouch's films are a

repudiation of intellectualism; their power stems from the sensuality of Rouch's cinematography. Rouch is a storyteller who fuses thought, action, and feeling to make an incontrovertible point: Songhay and Dogon, despite their lack of technological sophistication, understand unseen, inexplicable forces that most of us in the West have failed to grasp. These important points are never stated in the narration; they are evoked through the imagery and narrative force of his films.

Narrative Ethnography

An ethnography with a strong narrative presence can also be powerfully evocative. Ethnographic narratives, like ethnographic films, are not simply stories without disciplinary consequence. Narrative ethnographies usually underscore, albeit indirectly, themes of great theoretical importance. In fact, narrative ethnographies can be more attuned to the senses than ethnographic films; they, after all, can focus on smells and tastes as well as on sights and sounds. Narrative ethnographers also have the luxury of space to ponder at length the thoughts, feelings, and actions of their others—as well as their own.

In *Tales of the Field* John Van Maanen has placed what I call narrative ethnographies into two categories: impressionistic tales and literary tales. Just as impressionist painters like Monet used color, light, and form, among other things, to shock their audiences, so, Van Maanen claims, impressionist ethnographers, few of whom have published book-length works, try to awaken their audiences with startling stories. The literary tools these impressionist ethnographers use include: "words, metaphors, phrasings, imagery, and most importantly, the expansive recall of field-work experience."[33] These tales of recalled events are usually told in the first person, and often have the feel of a fast-paced novel. "Impressionistic writing tries to keep subject and object in constant view. The epistemological aim is then to braid the knower with the known."[34] These "impressionistic tales" are radically empirical, fusing thought, action, and sentiment without suffering the solipsism of many confessional texts.

Van Maanen distinguishes impressionist from literary tales. Both kinds of texts are much more likely to attract general audiences than the ethnographic confessional or the realist ethnography. Anthropologists, according to Van Maanen, generally don't write literary tales, which others call new journalism or cultural journalism. "Literary tales combine a reporter's sense of what is noteworthy (newsworthy) with a novelist's sense of narration. Dense characterization, dramatic plots, flashbacks (and flash-forwards), and alternative points of view are illustrative techniques."[35] All these techniques emotionally engage a broad audience, and the result is brisk sales of works that are often ethnographically significant and may encourage reticent professional ethnographers to improve their writing.[36]

Participation and Narrative Ethnography

There are a great many anthropologists, however, who will not leave the main highway. So mired are they in their "quest for certainty" that they move forward on the highway at a snail's pace. And even if they came upon the signpost,

```
Radical Empiricism Exit
        1 mile
```

they might not see it. And why not? There may well be institutional reasons. One is today rewarded more for theoretical than for descriptive contributions to the literature. My views about textual quality, which are spelled out in my own narrative ethnography, *In Sorcery's Shadow*, devolve from the depth of participation in the other's world. Put simply, the narrative depth of an ethnography is related directly to the nature of the author's participation in society. If a fieldworker attempts "participant observation," anthropology's most famous oxymoron, his or her disinterested stance will likely surface in a lifeless text. Lifeless texts constitute, I'm afraid, the large majority of anthropological works. They are often based on a relatively superficial penetration of the other's world and reflect the uncertainty of an author who attempts to participate and observe a phenomenon at the same time. More disquieting, however, are those lifeless texts written by anthropologists who have immersed themselves in the study of others. These men and women have compelling stories to tell, but recount them only in informal settings where it has been appropriate to reconnect thought with feeling and action.

Immersion or fuller participation in other worlds, however, can yield striking results. Take Jean Rouch's forty-five years of association with the Songhay of Niger. In his case, the spirits—in the bodies of mediums—told the great magicians of Wanzerbé to teach Rouch about Songhay sorcery and possession. In my case thirty years later, the spirits also paved the way for my entry into the world of Songhay sorcery. These powerful experiences steered Rouch onto the detour of film and me onto the detour of narrative ethnography. In both cases, we became apprentices—full participants in Songhay life. As apprentices our first lesson was: one is ignorant; one knows nothing. From that time on we built our knowledge; we continue to build it. Apprenticeship demands respect. "Without respect," Adamu Jeni-tongo once told me, "one learns nothing. You must always show us your respect." If there is one underlying theme in Rouch's films and in my books, it is that such a deep respect for other worlds and other ideas, ideas often preposterous to our own way of thinking, is central to the ethnographic endeavor.

This kind of respect demands a different kind of text or film; it is a text or film in which the sensuality of life is fused with the filmic or narrative image; the smells, the tastes, the sounds, the colors—lyrical and unsettling—of the land. This kind of respect, born of deep immersion in other worlds, demands that nameless informants be portrayed as recognizable individuals who suffer defeats and win victories in their social worlds. This kind of respect directs writers and filmmakers onto a radically empirical detour along which we can achieve the most simple yet most allusive goal of ethnography: to give our readers or viewers a *sense* of what it is like to live in other worlds, a taste of ethnographic things.

*   *   *

When we veer off the highway, we take many risks, for detours often lead us to distant, isolated places. And when we try to describe the wonders of these faraway places, many people don't want to listen. "Why did you go there?" "I've never heard of that place?" "Why did you wander so far off the path?" By taking the detour leading us toward a radically empirical anthropology, however, we will reach a destination where we will no longer have to write about writing ethnography; we will simply write our tales and sense that they are right.

Notes

INTRODUCTION. A RETURN TO THE SENSES

1. R. Burns, from the poem, "To a Mouse," in J. Kinsley (ed.), 1969: 102.

2. Differences in sensual biases between Europeans and Africans are noted in M. Wober, 1966: 182, who suggests that sensory patterns "may be predominantly visual in one culture, while in another culture, auditory or proprioceptive senses may have a much higher relative importance." Wober presents evidence suggesting that in African societies, especially those in southern Nigeria, the sensory biases are more auditory and proprioceptive than visual.

3. L. Rotkrug, 1981: 95.

4. D. Howes, 1988.

5. S. Langer, 1941: 13.

6. M. Foucault, 1975.

7. B. Malinowski, 1961: 108.

8. This orientation is found in A. Schutz, 1962.

9. These works include, among others, J. Clifford, 1988; J. Clifford and G. E. Marcus, 1986; G. E. Marcus and M. Fischer, 1985; and S. Tyler 1988.

10. A good example of such writing is S. Tyler, 1986: 45:

Post-modern experiments in ethnographic writing are the inverse of the modernist experiment. Where modernists sought by means of ideographic method to reveal the inner flow of thought hieroglyphically—as in Joyce or Pound, for example—post-modern writing focuses on the outer flow of speech, seeking not the thought that "underlies" speech, but the thought that *is* speech. Where modernists sought an identity between thought and language, post-modernists seek that "inner voice" which is the equivalent of thinking and speaking. Modernists sought a form of writing more in keeping with "things," emphasizing, in imitation of modern science, the descriptive function of writing—writing as a "picture of reality." This is not "realism" but "surrealism." Post-modern writing rejects this modernist *mimesis* in favor of a writing that "evokes" or "calls to mind," not by completion and similarity but by suggestion and difference.

CHAPTER 1. THE TASTE OF ETHNOGRAPHIC THINGS

1. Michel de Montaigne, [1580–88] 1943: 343.

2. The Songhay are a people of some 800,000 who live along the banks of the

Niger River from as far north as Timbucktu, Mali, to as far south as Sansane-Hausa in the Republic of Niger. There are also some 2.5 million first-language Songhay speakers living in Mali, Niger, and northern Benin. These Songhay speakers, however, are members of other ethnic groups (Wogo, Kurtey, Zerma, Dendi) which have distinct social histories. Djebo's family is from Say, a town on the west bank of the Niger some 200 kilometers south of Tillaberi; it was the center of Fulan power in the nineteenth century.

3. Seneca, [63–65 ACE] 1962, Book 2: 281.

4. V. Kahn, 1980: 1271.

5. *Ibid.:* 1269.

6. I. Kant, [1790] 1966: 32.

7. R. Williams, 1976.

8. *Ibid.:* 264.

9. M. de Montaigne, [1580–88] 1943: 320.

10. *Ibid.:* 345.

11. G. Ulmer, 1985: 52.

12. J. Derrida, 1974: 161.

13. J. Derrida, 1974: 109 as cited in Ulmer, 1985: 55.

14. G. Ulmer, 1985: 55.

15. G. E. Marcus and D. Cushman, 1982: 29.

16. P. Stoller 1984c: 102–03.

17. G. E. Marcus and D. Cushman, 1982: 31–36.

18. Some of the well-known contributions include J. Clifford, 1988; V. Crapanzano, 1980, 1985, 1987; J-P. Dumont, 1978; K. Dwyer, 1982; G. Marcus and M. Fischer, 1985; P. Rabinow, 1977; P. Stoller, 1984a, 1984b, 1986; P. Stoller and C. Olkes, 1987; D. Rose, 1987; S. Tyler, 1984, 1988.

19. J. Fabian, 1983: 164.

20. American Anthropological Association, 1984.

21. American Anthropological Association, 1985: 2.

22. I. C. Jarvie, 1975.

23. H. Dryfus and P. Rabinow, 1982: 107.

24. J. Agee, 1941: 139–40.

25. J. M. Chernoff, 1979: 39.

26. C. Geertz, 1973: 347.

27. C. Lévi-Strauss, [1955] 1974: 362.

28. M. Merleau-Ponty, 1964a: 159.

CHAPTER 2. EYE, MIND, AND WORD IN ANTHROPOLOGY

1. M. Merleau-Ponty, 1964a: 22.

2. G. Bachelard [1957] 1964 uses the term "reverberations" in his discussion of poetics. He suggests that the impact of a poem, for example, lies not in its referential content but in how this referential content carries a message that strikes a resonant chord ("reverberates") in the reader.

3. M. Merleau-Ponty, 1964a: 16.

4. G. Charbonnier, 1959, cited by Merleau-Ponty, 1964a: 31.

5. M. Foucault, 1963: IX.

6. See J. Favret-Saada, [1977] 1980; L. Peters, 1981; P. Stoller and C. Olkes, 1987.

7. Merleau-Ponty, 1964a: 25.

8. H. Lascault as cited in J. Cassou, 1968: 73.

9. R. P. Armstrong, 1971.

10. As explained in Chapter 1, Songhay society is characterized by social asymmetry. There are nobles who trace their descent patrilineally to Askia Mohammed Touré, King of the Songhay Empire from 1493 to 1527. There are free commoners

who have no patrilineal links to Askia Mohammed Touré. There are also descendants of (former) slaves who trace their descent patrilineally to prisoners of precolonial wars who were incorporated into Songhay society. And there are the foreigners, the aforementioned Wogo, Kurtey, Zerma, and Dendi (see Chapter 1, n. 2) as well as such groups as the Hausa, Tuareg, and Fulani. These peoples have migrated to and settled in Songhay over the centuries.

11. See P. Stoller, 1978, 1981.

12. A fuller treatment of these incidents is rendered in P. Stoller and C. Olkes' *In Sorcery's Shadow* (1987).

13. See P. Stoller, 1980.

14. *Ibid.*

15. M. Foucault, 1966.

16. G. E. Marcus and D. Cushman, 1982: 31.

17. M. L. Pratt, 1982: 140.

18. A. Moravia, 1972: 1. Consider two further examples of the "monarch-of-all-I-survey" convention of representation. The first is from Sir Richard Burton's *The Lake Regions of Central Africa* (1971): 307.

> Nothing, in sooth, could be more picturesque than this first view of the Tanganyika Lake, as it lay in the lap of the mountains, basking in the gorgeous tropical sunshine. Below and beyond a short foreground of rugged and precipitous hillfold, down which the footpath zigzags painfully, a narrow strip of emerald green, never sere and marvelously fertile, shelves towards a ribbon of glistening yellow sand, here bordered by sedgy rushes, there cleanly and clearly cut by the breaking wavelets.

The second example comes from Paul Theroux's *The Old Patagonian Express* (1978: 123:

> Guatemala City, an extremely horizontal place, is like a city on its back. Its ugliness, which has a threatened look (the low morose houses have earthquake cracks in their facades; the buildings wince at you with bright lines), is ugliest on those streets where, just past the last toppling house, a blue volcano cone bulges. I could see the volcanoes from the window of my hotel room. I was on the third floor, which was also the top floor.

In both cases, these excerpts, following Pratt's (1982: 149) arguments, use different stylistic devices—generated by the historical periods in which the works were written—to produce the rhetorical effect of seer over seen. Burton uses beauty and wonder to express his conquest of the lake; Moravia and Theroux use bizarre aesthetic juxtaposition to trivialize their descriptions.

19. M. L. Pratt, 1982: 152.

20. See pp. 25–26, and Chapter 1, n. 15.

21. A. N. Whitehead, 1969: 53.

22. R. Rorty, 1983.

23. F. de Saussure, [1915] 1959: 25.

24. C. Lévi-Strauss, 1967a: 549.

25. C. Lévi-Strauss as quoted in C. Geertz, 1973: 346.

26. G. E. Marcus and D. Cushman, 1982: 29.

27. R. Firth, [1936] 1959: 3.

28. S. Feld, 1982: 3.

29. See J. Clifford, 1988.

30. G. E. Marcus and D. Cushman, 1982: 47.

31. *Ibid.:* 48. See also P. Rabinow, 1977; J-P. Dumont, 1978; P. Riesman, 1977; V. Crapanzano, 1980, 1985; K. Dwyer, 1982; D. Rose, 1987; and P. Stoller and C. Olkes, 1987.

32. M. Foucault, 1966: 72.

33. N. Goodman, 1963: 32–33.

34. G. Hartmann, 1980: 150.

35. F. Nietzsche, [1876] 1956: 93.

36. M. Merleau-Ponty, 1968: 66.
37. *Ibid.:* 66.
38. *Ibid.:* 122–33.
39. M. Merleau-Ponty, 1964b: 139.
40. M. Merleau-Ponty, 1969: 20.
41. *Ibid.*

CHAPTER 3. "GAZING" AT THE SPACE OF SONGHAY POLITICS

1. A. N. Whitehead, 1969.
2. P. Stoller, 1978.
3. See P. Stoller, 1978, 1981; J-P. Olivier de Sardin, 1982, 1984.
4. See P. Stoller, 1978, 1980b.
5. P. Stoller, 1980b.
6. P. Stoller, 1978.
7. *Ibid.*
8. J. Duvignaud, 1969: 452.
9. M. Godelier, 1978.
10. M. Sahlins, 1972; J. Lizot, 1971.
11. G. Sjoberg, 1961: 96–97.
12. See H. Miner, 1966, R. Hull, 1976; and D. Gilmore, 1978.
13. C. Lévi-Strauss, 1967b: 128–59.
14. M. Griaule and G. Dieterlen, 1954.
15. R. Hull, 1976: 45.
16. See A. N. Whitehead, 1969; R. Rorty, 1979.
17. Aristotle, [ca. 335 BCE] 1961: 65–66.
18. A. Gurwitsch, 1978: 80–81.
19. P. Tempels, 1949.
20. M. Merleau-Ponty, 1964b: 47.
21. E. Husserl, [1931] 1960.
22. M. Merleau-Ponty, 1962: 243–44.
23. A. Schutz, 1962.

CHAPTER 4. SIGNS IN THE SOCIAL ORDER: RIDING A SONGHAY BUSH TAXI

1. This chapter is a hermeneutical analysis of the nature of anthropological understanding. My use of the term "sign" should not be taken as an intrinsic part of a strict semiological analysis of Songhay bush taxi interaction. Here I use the term to denote the presence of a fact, condition, or quality not immediately evident to an observer.

2. P. Ricoeur, 1979.

3. C. Geertz, 1973; K. Basso, 1979.

4. See J-P. Olivier de Sardan, 1982, 1984; P. Riesman, 1977; P. Stoller, 1978.

5. Tillaberi and Niamey are the major urban centers of the westernmost regions of the Republic of Niger. Most of the passengers boarding at Bonfebba, however, pass through Tillaberi en route to Niamey, a city of more than 400,000, which is also the capital of Niger.

6. While I have presented a corpus of interactional data in this chapter, my presentation and analysis of it do not fit within the conventional parameters of conversational analysis (see M. Schegloff, G. Jefferson, and H. Sachs, 1972; W. Labov, 1973; D. Sudnow, 1972). Here, interactional data are not seen as sources from which rules and/or structures can be induced, but rather as indications of deeper symbolic and metaphoric relationships that are central to a more profound comprehension of

the complexities of Songhay social life. In this light, my analysis is more akin to some of the earlier works of E. Goffman (1971, 1974).

7. P. Riesman pointed this out to me.

8. P. Ricoeur, 1979: 79.

9. "Saying" refers to metacommunicative action. As G. Bateson (1972), among others, has pointed out, the utterance of a simple sentence may carry any number of metacommunicative messages, some of which are deeper than others.

10. G. Bachelard, [1957] 1964.

11. *Ibid.:* xv.

12. J. Edie, 1976: 151.

13. J. D. Sapir, 1977: 6.

14. B. Beck, 1978: 83.

15. J. Fernandez, 1977: 100–02.

16. N. Goodman, 1963: 80.

17. M. Johnson and G. Lakoff, 1980.

18. M. Black, 1962.

19. R. P. Armstrong, 1980: 77–78.

20. P. Stoller, 1977.

21. In the Songhay language there exist a set of expressions such as *Ni manti fala* (literally, "You are not easy"), which means in context "You are hard," and *hal manti mosso* (lit., "until not a little"), which means "a whole lot" or "very much." One therefore finds a sentence such a *A ga ba ni hal manti mosso* (lit., "I like you until not a little"), which in context means "I like you a whole lot."

22. See R. F. Thompson, 1974; J. Fernandez, 1977; B. Beck, 1978.

23. See P. Stoller, 1980b.

24. See P. Stoller, 1981.

25. P. Ricoeur, 1979: 100.

26. See E. Albert, 1972; D. Hymes, 1974.

27. P. Ricoeur, 1967: 71.

CHAPTER 5. SON OF ROUCH: SONGHAY VISIONS OF THE OTHER

1. The chain-swallowing episode occurs in the second part of the film. The sohancis gather for a dance. As their dancing to the sound of the tam-tam becomes frenzied, one man goes into trance and vomits his *sisiri*, his magical chain that materializes during these trances. The chain is the manifestation of his power as a sorcerer.

According to the late Sohanci Adamu Jenitongo, only a few sorcerers receive these chains. A sohanci receives a chain when his master prepares for him a paste which is eaten. When the sohanci enters into a trance, the paste is transformed into a chain that is vomited and swallowed. In some circumstances, the chain is passed from a dying sorcerer to his successor. Just as he is about to die, the master sohanci vomits his chain and tells his successor to swallow it. In this way the chain is passed from one generation to the next.

2. See J. Rouch, [1971] 1978.

3. *Ibid.*

4. J. Rouch, 1960: 5.

5. *Ibid.:* 6.

6. Other aspects of this trip to Wanzerbé in 1977 are explored in P. Stoller and C. Olkes, 1987.

7. See M. Griaule, 1957; J. Clifford, 1988.

8. See P. Stoller 1984c; P. Stoller and C. Olkes, 1987.

9. See D. Kondo, 1986; V. Crapanzano, 1980; E. Bruner, 1986. Recent articles on the reflexivity of anthropological fieldwork reflect brilliantly the complexity of

doing ethnography. Feld (1987: 191) has engaged in what he calls "dialogic editing," which is "the impact of Kaluli voices on what I tell you about them in my voice; how their take on my take on them requires reframing and refocusing on my part." And yet,

> Whatever we write, whatever we speak, whatever we perform, whatever we render through music, film, poetry, holography, or some sort of computer language, precipitates a difference—a counter-rendition or its possibility at least—that despite all our efforts to encompass will always (in both its contemporary sense of escape and its etymological one of play) elude us. . . . The point is that we and they—the transform of the I and you of the field encounter—can never be fully specified (Crapanzano 1987: 188–89).

Crapanzano is correct. We can no longer seriously seek to represent the Other's reality in our texts; rather we must attempt to describe as faithfully as possible the textures of their lives in their worlds. Crapanzano is one of the few anthropologists whose ethnographic works, in which he takes considerable professional risks, reflect this orientation to the world. More of us need to follow his lead, risking vilification for potentially brilliant failures of ethnographic description. Crapanzano's point is further reinforced by V. Y. Mudimbe (1988) who discusses brilliantly how discourses about (African) reality have been invented and reinvented.

10. S. Scarr, 1985: 499.
11. See A. N. Kanya-Forstner, 1969; I. Kimba, 1981; J-P. Olivier de Sardan, 1984.
12. See J-P. Olivier de Sardan, 1969, 1976, 1984; P. Stoller, 1981, 1984a.
13. M. Klein and R. Roberts, 1980: 393.
14. See I. Kimba, 1981; J-P. Olivier de Sardan, 1984.
15. C. De Brosses, 1760; J. Gobineau, [1853–55], 1967.
16. J. Bousset, 1836; as cited and translated by C. Miller 1985: 42.
17. H. Cole, 1981.
18. U. Beier, 1964.
19. J. Rouch, 1960: 74–75.
20. I. Wallerstein, 1984; J. Comaroff, 1985.
21. S. Scarr, 1985: 499.
22. R. Wagner, 1981.
23. See J. Dewey, [1929] 1980a, [1934] 1980b; W. James, [1909] 1978.
24. J-F. Lyotard, [1979] 1984: 4.
25. See I. Wallerstein, 1984.
26. A particularly pernicious example of this kind of writing is J. W. Beul's *Heroes of the Dark Continent* [1889] 1971.
27. Olson's Travelworld, 1986.
28. Edward Said's *Orientalism* (1978) has inspired a number of studies of the imagery that western writers, Africanists, use to portray Africans. The most recent is Miller's *Blank Darkness: Africanist Discourse in French* (1985).
29. V. S. Naipaul, 1984: 530.
30. Historical themes are expressed dramatically during Songhay possession ceremonies. These themes are embedded in the music, dance, ritual objects, and words of possession ceremonies. History is also re-enacted during Islamic ceremonies—holidays, births, marriages, deaths—when bards recite epic poetry and the genealogies of local nobles, all of whom are descendants of Askia Mohammed Touré.

CHAPTER 6. SOUND IN SONGHAY POSSESSION

1. See M. Foucault, 1975.
2. See W. Ong, 1967; J. Goody, 1977.
3. V. Zuckerkandl, 1956.
4. *Ibid.:* 70.
5. M. Foucault, 1975: 3.

6. In *Sound and Symbol* (1956) Zuckerkandl distinguishes sound from tone. If I am interpreting his text correctly, he associates tone with music, which is, of course, distinct from other kinds of sounds (words, noise, etc.). Given the existential perspective of this chapter, I would extend Zuckerkandl's musical stance toward the universe to praise-poetry and ritual incantations (see Chapter 7, especially). In my view the sounds of praise-songs or ritual incantations carry the same forces and qualities which Zuckerkandl ascribes to the music of the tonal world.

7. V. Zuckerkandl, 1956: 68.

8. *Ibid.:* 69.

9. *Ibid.:* 71.

10. S. Feld, 1982: 3.

11. See A. Jackson, 1968; R. Needham, 1968; W. Sturtevant, 1968.

12. In general, possession emerges during times of social crisis and change. Olivier de Sardan (1982) suggests that Songhay possession dates to Askia Mohammed Touré, who attempted to Islamize the Songhay empire. Such a move undermined the locally-based lineage as the principal governing body of Songhay society; it also lessened the importance of the lineage religion, which was based upon making sacrifices to the lineage ancestors. Songhay possession emerged, or so it is believed, during this time of great sociocultural and religious upheaval. See also Stoller (1989).

13. See J. Rouch, 1960; P. Stoller, 1989.

14. See P. Stoller, 1989.

15. *Ibid.*

16. *Ibid.*

17. B. Surugue, 1972: 29.

18. The string of the godji is plucked from only two of the many kinds of horses found in Songhay. These are the *sobe* and the *guro*, which are distinguished by the color of their bodies and their feet. These horses, in fact, are mentioned in the following praise-song, which is recited by a *sorko*, at a possession dance:
Sobe hamno a min Kalam bisa a min Ouallam bisa.
"The hair of the sobe will not pass Kalam or Ouallan [two centers of intense possession activity]."
Guro hamni a min Kalam bisa a min Ouallam bisa.
"The hair of the guro will not pass. . . ."

19. Sohanci Adamu Jenitongo, personal communication.

20. *Ibid.* See also P. Stoller, 1989.

21. See T. Hale, 1982: 4; also M. Kati 1911; D. T. Niani, 1965; G. Innes, 1974; and J. W. Johnson, 1986.

22. J. T. Irvine, 1980: 6.

23. *Ibid:* 7.

24. V. Zuckerkandl, 1956.

25. C. Keil, 1979.

26. J. M. Chernoff, 1979: 31.

27. E. Basso, 1985: 311.

CHAPTER 7. SOUND IN SONGHAY SORCERY

1. In the Songhay view of the world, the human body consists of flesh (*ga*), life force (*hundi*), and the double (*bia*). The witch (*cerkaw*) has the capacity to steal a person's double. When this occurs, usually after a frightful confrontation during the night, the bewitched person becomes ill, suffering from chronic fatigue, nausea, and diarrhea. The symptoms are the results of the bewitched person's loss of bia. Typically, the witch will find a hiding place for a victim's double. The symptoms associated with witchcraft continue until a sorko intervenes and helps to return the double to its human counterpart, or until the witch transforms the double into a

sacrificial animal and slits the animal's throat. When this sacrifice occurs, the bewitched person dies. See P. Stoller and C. Olkes, 1987.

2. Sorko Djibo Mounmouni, Mehanna, April, 1977.
3. See S. Freud, 1913; S. Tambiah, 1968.
4. See J. L. Austin, 1962; J. Searle, 1968.
5. S. Tambiah, 1968: 175.
6. *Ibid.:* 215.
7. *Ibid.:* 185.
8. *Ibid.:* 202.
9. M. Foucault, 1970.
10. W. Ong, 1967: 113.
11. P. Riesman, 1977: 148.
12. G. Lienhardt, 1961: 236.
13. J. Favret-Saada, [1977] 1980: 9–10.
14. See C. Keil, 1979; J. M. Chernoff, 1979.
15. See J. Boulnois and B. Hama, 1953; J. Rouch, 1953, 1960; J. O. Hunwick, 1966, 1972, 1985.
16. J. Rouch, 1960: 47.
17. See P. Stoller, 1989.
18. See P. Stoller and C. Olkes, 1987; P. Stoller, 1989.
19. See P. Stoller and C. Olkes, 1987.
20. V. Zuckerkandl, 1956: 364.
21. *Ibid.:* 364.
22. *Ibid.:* 364.
23. M. Merleau-Ponty, 1968.
24. V. Zuckerkandl, 1956: 364.
25. *Ibid.:* 366.
26. See P. Riesman, 1977; G. Lienhardt, 1961; J. Favret-Saada, 1980; J. T. Irvine, 1980.
27. See C. Keil, 1979.
28. Sorko Djibo Mounmouni, Mehanna, April, 1977.

CHAPTER 8. THE RECONSTRUCTION OF ETHNOGRAPHY

1. See P. Stoller and C. Olkes, 1987 for a full description of the Songhay world of eternal war.
2. C. Lévi-Strauss, 1967: 161–81.
3. D. Hume, [1777] 1902, vol. 1, part 4, sec. 1.
4. This chapter concerns the broad philosophical underpinnings (as opposed to the strictly visual underpinnings discussed in Chapter 2) of anthropology as they are reflected in anthropological discourse. A growing literature—an excellent literature—discusses ethnographies as texts. The works of Marcus and Cushman (1982) Marcus and Fischer (1985), and Clifford 1988), for example, discuss indirectly the anthropological episteme. They consider such topics as ethnographic realism, the authority of ethnographic texts, the displaced authority of experimental ethnographic texts, ethnographic rhetoric, and the relationship between the writers and readers of ethnography. My focus here is similar but broader. Instead of considering style, form, or ethnographic rhetoric directly, my interest lies in the epistemological constraints that govern institutional judgments of anthropological writing. More expositions, especially historical ones, are needed. See also C. Geertz (1984).
5. M. Foucault, 1980: 197.
6. M. Foucault, 1970: 399.
7. Heraclitus as translated in M. Heidegger, 1975: 75.
8. See R. Rorty, 1979, 1983.
9. F. de Saussure, [1915] 1959: 9.

10. *Ibid.:* 9.
11. *Ibid.:* 9.
12. *Ibid.:* 9.
13. C. Lévi-Strauss, 1969: 478–79.
14. C. Lévi-Strauss as quoted in C. Geertz, 1973: 346.
15. See A. R. Radcliffe-Brown, 1953.
16. D. Hymes, 1974: 35.
17. *Ibid.:* 43.
18. M. Agar and J. Hobbs, 1983: 33.
19. M. Agar, 1982: 779.
20. See S. Diamond, 1974: 172–74.
21. See J. Derrida, 1976.
22. See S. Langer, 1942; M. Merleau-Ponty, 1964a.
23. See D. Tedlock, 1982; E. Said, 1975. My "sludge list" of anthropological writing is undoubtedly skewed or unrepresentative, since I selected from the beginnings of journal articles or books. I selected these beginnings deliberately; with Said, I believe beginnings are rhetorically and philosophically significant. They are intentional. Lyrical, revelatory beginnings reflect, generally, a humanistic or critical interpretation to follow. Beginnings with theoretical contentions or general assumptions, by contrast, signal a more positivistic approach. My own view, of course, is preliminary.
24. A. J. Osborn, 1983: 563.
25. D. White, M. Burton, and M. Dow, 1981: 824.
26. F. Kaplan, and D. M. Levine, 1981: 869.
27. G. White and C. Prachuabhmoh, 1982: 2.
28. D. J. Austin, 1983: 223.
29. G. Appell, 1983: 202.
30. J. T. Irvine, 1982: 31.
31. P. Stoller, 1977: 31.
32. S. Diamond, 1974: 93.
33. R. Firth, [1936] 1959: 3.
34. M. Lambek, 1981.
35. J. M. Chernoff, 1979.
36. V. Crapanzano, 1973.
37. V. Crapanzano, 1985.
38. J. Favret-Saada, 1980: 3–4.
39. C. Lévi-Strauss as cited in C. Geertz, 1973: 346.
40. *Ibid.* H. Ross, 1982: 5.
41. *Ibid.:* 6.
42. Plato as cited in S. Diamond, 1974: 187.
43. M. Merleau-Ponty, 1968.
44. M. Heidegger, 1971: 57–58.
45. J. Favret-Saada and J. Contreras, 1981.
46. D. Hume, [1777] 1902: vol. 1, part 4, sec. 1.
47. G. Spivak, 1976: xix.
48. M. Agar, 1982: 779.
49. *Ibid.:* 779.
50. J. W. Fernandez, 1982: M. Jackson, 1986; D. Rose, 1987.

CHAPTER 9. DETOURS

1. This is a term used by Mary Louise Pratt (1982) to denote a set of literary conventions used by writers during a variety of literary epochs. See also Chapter 2.
2. The surrealist assumption that Leiris employed in *Afrique fantôme* was to write a journal as a first, immediate impression—automatic writing. As a consequence, the first draft and published version of the book are virtually identical.

3. J. Favret-Saada, 1980.
4. See R. Bernstein, 1976; see also Chapters 1 and 2.
5. E. Goffman, 1981: 74.
6. J. Dewey, [1934] 1980: 32.
7. *Ibid.:* 33.
8. *Ibid.:* 33.
9. R. Rorty, 1979: 1.
10. *Ibid.:* 2.
11. *Ibid.:* 42–43.
12. *Ibid.:* 269.
13. See M. Agar, 1982.
14. W. James, [1909] 1978: 100.
15. R. Rorty, 1979: 361.
16. *Ibid.:* 370.
17. See E. Said, 1984.
18. C. Tisdale, 1979: 101.
19. *Ibid.:* 104–05.
20. *Ibid.:* 72.
21. *Ibid.:* 72.
22. J. Burnham, 1974: 139.
23. R. Barthes, 1972: 164–65.
24. G. Ulmer, 1985: 232.
25. See D. Hiley, 1988.
26. See J. Berger, 1965; H. Richter, 1980; H. Read, 1972; A. Breton, 1969, 1973; L. Lippard, 1970.
27. See M. Foucault, 1970, 1980; J. Derrida, 1976; J-F. Lyotard, [1979] 1984, 1986.
28. J. Dewey, [1934] 1980: 33.
29. *Ibid.:* 46.
30. *Ibid.:* 34.
31. See J. Dewey, [1929] 1980a; see also G. Marcus and M. Fischer, 1985; J. Clifford, 1988; J. Clifford and G. Marcus, 1986; S. Tyler, 1988.
32. See P. Stoller, 1988.
33. J. Van Maanen, 1988: 102.
34. *Ibid.:* 103.
35. *Ibid.:* 132.
36. *Ibid.:* 132.

References Cited

Agar, M.
  1982 Toward an ethnographic language. *American Anthropologist* 84: 779–96.
Agar, M. and J. Hobbs
  1983 Natural plans: using AI planning in the analysis of ethnographic interviews. *Ethos* 11:33–49.
Agee, J.
  1941 *Let us now praise famous men.* Boston: Houghton-Mifflin.
Albert, E.
  1972 Cultural patterning of speech behavior in Burundi. In J. J. Gumperz and D. Hymes (eds.) *Directions in sociolinguistics: The ethnography of communication.* New York: Holt, Rinehart and Winston. 72–106.
American Anthropological Association
  1984 Title page and abstract for publication. *Anthropology Newsletter* 25 (1): 12D.
Appell, G.
  1983 Methodological problems with concepts of corporation, corporate social grouping, and cognatic descent group. *American Ethnologist* 10: 302–13.
Aristotle
  [ca. 335 BCE] 1961 *Physics.* Richard Hope, transl. Lincoln: University of Nebraska Press.
Armstrong, R. P.
  1971 *The affecting presence: An essay in humanistic anthropology.* Urbana: University of Illinois Press.
Austin, D. J.
  1983 Culture and ideology in the English-speaking Caribbean. *American Ethnologist* 10: 223–41.

Austin, J. L.
 1962 *How to do things with words*. London: Oxford University Press.
Bachelard, G.
 [1957] 1964 *The poetics of space*. New York: Orion Press.
Barthes, R.
 1972 To write: An intransitive verb. In R. and F. DeGeorge (eds.) *The structuralists from Marx to Lévi-Strauss*. Garden City, N.Y.: Doubleday: 164–72.
Basso, E.
 1985 *A musical view of the universe: Kalapalo myth and ritual performances*. Philadelphia: University of Pennsylvania Press.
Basso, K.
 1979 *Portraits of "the whiteman." Linguistic play and cultural symbols among the Western Apache*. New York: Cambridge University Press.
Bateson, G.
 1972 *Steps to an ecology of mind*. New York: Ballantine Books.
Beck, B. E. F.
 1978 Metaphor as a mediator between the semantic and analogic modes of thought. *Current Anthropology* 19: 83–88.
Beier, U.
 1964 Gelede. *Nigeria Magazine* 175: 3–15.
Berger, J.
 1965 *The success and failure of Picasso*. London: Penguin.
Bernstein, R.
 1976 *The restructuring of social and political theory*. Philadelphia: University of Pennsylvania Press.
Beul, J. W.
 [1889] 1971 *Heros of the dark continent*. Freeport, N.Y.: Books for Libraries Press.
Black, M.
 1962 *Models and metaphors*. Ithaca, N.Y.: Cornell University Press.
Boulnois, J. and B. Hama
 1953 *L'Empire de Gao: Histoire, coûtumes et magie des Songhai*. Paris: Maisonneuve.
Bousset, J.
 1836 *Oeuvres compléts*. Paris. Lefevre.
Breton, A.
 1969 *Manifesto of surrealism*. Trans. R. Sears and H. R. Lane. Ann Arbor: University of Michigan Press.
 1973 *Surrealism and painting*. New York: Harper and Row.
Bruner, E. (ed.)
 1986 *Text, play, story: The construction and reconstruction of self and society*. Washington, D.C.: American Anthropological Association.
Burnham, J.
 1974 *Great western salt works*. New York: G. Brazillier.
Burton, R. F.
 1971 *The lake regions of Central Africa*. St. Clair Shores, Mi.: The Scholarly Press.

Cassou, J.
  1968   *Art and confrontation.* New York: New York Graphic Art Society.
Charbonnier, G.
  1959   *Le monologue du peintre.* Paris: Julliard.
Chernoff, J. M.
  1979   *African rhythm and African sensibility.* Chicago: University of Chicago Press.
Clifford, J.
  1988   *The predicament of culture.* Cambridge, Ma.: Harvard University Press.
Clifford, J. and G. E. Marcus (eds.)
  1986   *Writing culture: the poetics and politics of ethnography.* Berkeley: University of California Press.
Cole, H.
  1981   *Mbari.* Bloomington: Indiana University Press.
Comaroff, J.
  1985   *Body of power, spirit of resistance.* Chicago: University of Chicago Press.
Crapanzano, V.
  1973   *The Hamshada.* Berkeley: University of California Press.
  1980   *Tuhami: Portrait of a Moroccan.* Chicago: University of Chicago Press.
  1985   *Waiting: The whites of South Africa.* New York: Random House.
  1987   Editorial. *Cultural Anthropology* 2: 179–89.
De Brosses, J.
  1760   *Du culte des dieux fétiches, ou parallel de l'ancienne religion de l'Egypte avec la religion actuelle de Nigritie.* Paris: n.p.
Derrida, J.
  1974   *Glas.* Paris: Galilée.
  1976   *Of grammatology.* Trans. G. T. Spivak. Baltimore: The Johns Hopkins University Press.
Dewey, J.
  [1929] 1980a   *The quest for certainty.* New York: Perigee Books.
  [1934] 1980b.   *Art as experience.* New York: Perigee Books.
Diamond, S.
  1974   *In search of the primitive.* London: Transaction Books.
Dryfus, H. and P. Rabinow
  1982   *Michel Foucault: Beyond structuralism and hermeneutics.* Chicago: University of Chicago Press.
Dumont, J-P.
  1978   *The headman and I.* Austin: University of Texas Press.
Duvignaud, J.
  1969   Vivent les sauvauges! *La nouvelle revue francaise* 195: 449–52.
Dwyer, K.
  1982   *Moroccan dialogues.* Baltimore: The Johns Hopkins University Press.
Edie, J.
  1976   *Speaking and meaning: The phenomenology of language.* Bloomington: Indiana University Press.

Fabian, J.
   1983   *Time and the other*. New York: Columbia University Press.
Favret-Saada, J.
   [1977] 1980   *Deadly words: Witchcraft in the Bocage*. London: Cambridge University Press.
Favret-Saada, J. and J. Contreras
   1981   *Corps pour corps: Enquête sur la sorcellérie dans le Bocage*. Paris: Gallimard.
Feld, S.
   1982   *Sound and sentiment: Birds, weeping, poetics, and song in Kaluli expression*. Philadelphia: University of Pennsylvania Press.
   1987   Dialogic editing. *Cultural Anthropology* 2: 191–215.
Fernandez, J. W.
   1977   The performance of ritual metaphors. In J. D. Sapir and J. C. Crocker (eds.) *The social use of metaphor: Essays on the anthropology of rhetoric*. Philadelphia: University of Pennsylvania Press. 100–131.
   1982   *Bwiti*. Princeton, N.J.: Princeton University Press.
Firth, R.
   [1936] 1959   *We, the Tikopia*. Boston: Beacon Press.
Foucault, M.
   1963   *Naissance de la clinique: Une archéaologie du régard médicale*. Paris: PUF.
   1966   *Les mots et les choses: Une archéaologie des sciences humaines*. Paris: Gallimard.
   1970   *The order of things. An archaeology of the human sciences*. New York: Random House.
   1975   *The birth of the clinic*. New York: Random House.
   1980   *Power/knowledge*. New York: Pantheon.
Freud, S.
   1913   *Totem and taboo*. London: Hogarth Press.
Geertz, C.
   1973   *The interpretation of cultures*. New York: Basic Books.
   1984   Anti-anti relativism. *American Anthropologist* 86: 263–78.
Gilmore, D.
   1977   The social organization of space: Class, cognition, and space in a Spanish town. *American Ethnologist* 4: 437–53.
Gobineau, Joseph de.
   [1853–55] 1967   *Essai sur l'inégalité des races humaines*. Paris: Pierre Belfond.
Godelier, M.
   1978   *Perspectives on Marxist anthropology*. London: Cambridge University Press.
Goffman, E.
   1971   *Relations in public*. New York: Harper Colophon.
   1974   *Frame analysis: An essay on the organization of experience*. New York: Harper Colophon.
   1981   *Forms of talk*. Philadelphia: University of Pennsylvania Press.
Goodman, N.
   1963   *The languages of art*. Indianapolis: Hackett Publications.

Goody, J.
  1977   *The domestication of the savage mind.* London: Cambridge University Press.
Griaule, M.
  1957   *Methode de l'ethnographie.* Paris: PUF.
Griaule, M., and G. Dieterlen
  1954   The Dogon of the French Sudan. In D. Forde (ed.) *African worlds.* London: Oxford University Press: 83–111.
Gurwitsch, A.
  1978   Galilean physics in the light of Husserl's phenomenology. In T. Luckmann (ed.) *Phenomenology and sociology.* Middlesex, England: Penguin: 71–90.
Hale, T.
  1982   Kings, scribes and bards: A look at songs of survival for keepers of the oral tradition among the Songhay-speaking peoples of Niger. Paper presented at the First International Congress of African Folklore, Budapest.
Hartmann, G.
  1980   *Criticism in the wilderness.* New Haven, Conn.: Yale University Press.
Heidegger, M.
  1971   *On the way to language.* New York: Harper and Row.
  1975   *Early Greek thinking.* New York: Harper and Row.
Hiley, D.
  1988   *Philosophy in question: Essays on a Pyrrhonian theme.* Chicago: University of Chicago Press.
Howes, D.
  1988   On the odour of the soul: Spatial representation and olfactory classification in Eastern Indonesia and Western Melanesia. *Bijdragen* 144: 84–113.
Hull, R.
  1976   *African cities and towns before the european conquest.* New York: W. W. Norton.
Hume, D.
  [1777] 1902   *Enquiries concerning human understanding.* Oxford: Clarendon Press.
Hunwick, J. O.
  1966   Religion and state in the Songhay empire. In I. M. Lewis (ed.) *Islam in tropical Africa.* London: Oxford University Press: 296–316.
  1972   Songhay, Bornu, and Hausaland in the sixteenth century. In J. F. Ajayi and M. Crowder (eds.) *History of West Africa,* Vol. 1. New York: Columbia University Press: 264–302.
  1985   *Askia Mohammed.* London: Oxford University Press.
Husserl, E.
  [1931] 1960   *Cartesian meditations.* The Hague: Marcus Nijhoff.
Hymes, D.
  1974   *Foundations in sociolinguistics: An ethnographic approach.* Philadelphia: University of Pennsylvania Press.

Innes, G.
1974   *Sunjata: Three Mande versions.* London: School of Oriental and African Studies.
Irvine, J. T.
1980   Address as magic and rhetoric: Praise-naming in West Africa. Paper presented at the 79th Annual Meeting of the American Anthropological Association.
1982   The communication of affect. In H. Brynes (ed.) *Contemporary perceptions of language: Interdisciplinary dimensions.* Washington, D. C.: Georgetown University Press: 31–47.
Jackson, A.
1968   Sound and ritual. *Man* (NS)3: 293–300.
Jackson, M.
1986   *Barawa or the way birds fly in the sky.* Washington, D.C.: Smithsonian Institution Press.
James, William
[1909] 1978   *Pragmatism and the meaning of truth.* Cambridge, Ma.: Harvard University Press.
Jarvie, I. C.
1975   Epistle to the Anthropologists. *American Anthropologist* 77: 253–67.
Johnson, J. W.
1986   *The epic of Sunjata.* Bloomington: Indiana University Press.
Johnson, M. and G. Lakoff
1980   *Metaphors we live by.* Chicago: University of Chicago Press.
Kahn, V.
1980   The sense of taste in Montaigne's essays. *MLN* 95: 1269–91.
Kant, I.
[1790] 1966   *The critique of judgment.* New York: Hafner Publishing Co.
Kanya-Forstner, A. N.
1969   *The conquest of the Western Soudan.* London: Cambridge University Press.
Kaplan F. and D. M. Levine
1981   Cognitive mapping of a folk taxonomy of Mexican pottery: A multivariate approach. *American Anthropologist* 83: 868–85.
Kati, M.
1911   *Tarikh al fattach.* Paris: Maisonneuve.
Keil, C.
1979   *Tiv song.* Chicago: University of Chicago Press.
Kimba, I.
1981   *Guerres et sociétés.* Etudes Nigeriennes #48. Niamey: Unversité de Niamey.
Kinsley, J. (ed.)
1969   Robert Burns: Poems and songs. London: Oxford University Press.
Klein, M. and R. Roberts
1980   The Bamana slave exodus in 1905 and the decline of slavery in the Western Soudan. *Journal of African History* 21: 375–95.
Kondo, D.
1986   Dissolution and reconstruction of self: Implications for anthropological epistemology. *Cultural Anthropology* 1: 74–89.

Labov, W.
1972 *Language in the inner city: Studies in the Black English vernacular.* Philadelphia: University of Pennsylvania Press.
Lambek, M.
1981 *Human spirits.* London: Cambridge University Press.
Langer, S.
1942 *Philosophy in a new key.* Cambridge, Ma.: Harvard University Press.
Leiris, M.
[1934] 1985 *Afrique fantôme.* Paris: Gallimard.
Lévi-Strauss, C.
1967a *Les structures élémentaires de la parenté.* Paris-Le Haye: Mouton.
1967b *Structural anthropology.* Garden City, N.Y. Doubleday.
[1955] 1973 *Tristes tropiques.* J. and D. Weightman, transl. New York: Atheneum.
1969 *The elementary forms of kinship.* Boston: Beacon Press.
Lienhardt, G.
1961 *Divinity and experience: the religion of the Dinka.* London: Oxford University Press.
Lippard, L. (ed.)
1970 *Surrealists on art.* Englewood Cliffs, N.J.: Prentice-Hall.
Lizot, J.
1971 Economie ou société? Quelque thèmes à propos d'une étude d'une communauté d'Amerindien. *Journal de la Société des Americanistes* 60: 137–75.
Lyotard, J-F.
[1979] 1984 *The postmodern condition.* Minneapolis: University of Minnesota Press.
1986 *Le postmodernism expliqué aux enfants.* Paris: Galilée.
Malinowski, B.
[1922] 1961 *Argonauts of the western pacific.* New York: Dutton.
Marcus, G. E. and D. Cushman
1982 Ethnographies as texts. *Annual Reviews of Anthropology* 11: 25–69.
Marcus, G. E. and M. Fischer
1985 *Anthropology as cultural critique.* Chicago: University of Chicago Press.
Merleau-Ponty, M.
1962 *The phenemonology of perception.* London: Routledge and Kegan Paul.
1964a *L'Oeil et l'esprit.* Paris: Gallimard.
1964b *Le Visible et l'invisible.* Paris: Gallimard.
1969 *The prose of the world.* Evanston, Il.: Northwestern University Press.
Miller, C.
1985 *Blank darkness: Africanist discourse in French.* Chicago: University of Chicago Press.
Miner, H.
1966 *The primitive city of Timbucktoo.* New York: Anchor Books.
Montaigne, M. de.
[1580–88] 1943 *Selected essays.* New York: Walter Black.

Moravia, A.
1972 *Which tribe do you belong to?* New York: Farrar, Strauss and Giroux.
Mudimbe, V. Y.
1988 *The invention of Africa: Gnosis, philosophy and the order of knowledge.* Bloomington: Indiana University Press.
Naipaul, V. S.
1984 The crocodiles of Yamoussoukro. *The New Yorker,* May 14: 52–119.
Needham, R.
1968 Percussion and transition. *Man* (NS)2: 606–14.
Niani, D. T.
1965 *Sunjata: An epic of old Mali.* London: Longman.
Nietzsche, F.
[1876] 1956 *The birth of tragedy out of the spirit of music.* Francis Groffling, transl. Garden City, N.Y.: Doubleday, Anchor Books.
Olivier de Sardan, J-P.
1969 *Les Voleurs d'hommes.* Paris: Institut d'Ethnologie.
1976 *Quand nos pères étaient captifs.* Paris: Nubia.
1982 *Concepts et conceptions Zarma-Songhay.* Paris: Nubia.
1984 *Sociétés Songay-Zarma.* Paris: Karthala.
Olson's Travelworld
1986 *Africa, Travelworld 1986.* London: Olson's Travel World, Inc.
Ong, W.
1967 *The presence of the word.* New Haven, Conn.: Yale University Press.
Osborn, A. J.
1983 Ecological aspects of equestrian adaptations in aboriginal North America. *American Anthropologist* 85: 563–92.
Peters, L.
1981 *Ecstasy and healing in Nepal.* Malibu: Udena Publications.
Pratt, M. L.
1982 Conventions of representation: Where discourse and ideology meet. In H. Byrnes (ed.) *Contemporary perceptions of language: Interdisciplinary dimensions.* Washington, D.C.: Georgetown University Press. 139–56.
Rabinow, P.
1977 *Reflections on fieldwork in Morocco.* Berkeley: University of California Press.
Radcliffe-Brown, A. R.
1953 *Structure and function in primitive society.* Chicago: University of the Chicago Press.
Read, H.
1972 *Surrealism.* New York: Praeger.
Richter, H.
1970 *Dada: Art and anti-art.* New York: Abrams.
Ricoeur, P.
1967 Le problème du 'double' sens comme problème herméneutique et comme problème semantique. *Cahiers Internationaux de Symbolisme* 6: 56–71.
1979 The model of the text: Meaningful action considered as a text. In R. Rabinow and W. Sullivan (eds.) *Interpretive social science: A reader.* Berkeley: University of California Press: 73–101.

Riesman, P.
1977 *Freedom in Fulani social life.* Chicago: University of Chicago Press.

Rorty, R.
1979 *Philosophy and the mirror of nature.* Princeton, N.J.: Princeton University Press.
1983 Relativism (Howison Lecture at the University of California, Berkeley, Jan. 31, 1983).

Rose, D.
1987 *Black American street life: South Philadelphia, 1969–1971.* Philadelphia: University of Pennsylvania Press.

Ross, H.
1982 Human linguistics. In H. Byrnes (ed.) *Contemporary perceptions of language: Interdisciplinary dimensions.* Washington, D.C.: Georgetown University Press. 1–30.

Rotkrug, L.
1981 The "odour of sanctity" and the Hebrew origins of christian relic veneration. *Historical Reflections/Reflections Historiques* 8: 95–137.

Rouch, J.
1953 *Contribution à l'étude de l'histoire Songhay.* Memoire #29. Dakar: I.F.A.N.
1960 *La religion et la magie Songhay.* Paris: PUF.
[1971] 1978 On the vicissitudes of the self: The possessed dancer, the magician, the sorcerer, the filmmaker, and the ethnographer. *Studies in the Anthropology of Visual Communication* 4: 2–8.

Sahlins, M.
1972 *Stoneage economics.* New York: Columbia University Press.

Said, E.
1975 *Beginnings.* New York: Basic Books.
1978 *Orientalism.* New York: Basic Books.
1984 *The world, the text, the critic.* Cambridge, Ma.: Harvard University Press.

Sapir, J. D.
1977 The anatomy of metaphor. In J. D. Sapir and J. C. Crocker (eds.) *The social uses of metaphor.* Philadelphia: University of Pennsylvania Press. 3–33.

Saussure, F. de.
[1915] 1955 *Course in general linguistics.* New York: Philosophical Library.

Scarr, S.
1985 Constructing psychology: Making facts and fables for our times. *American Psychologist* 40: 499–512.

Schegloff, E., G. Jefferson, and H. Sacks
1972 The preference for self-correction in the organization of repair in conversation. *Language* 53: 361–82.

Schutz, A.
1962 *Collected papers I: The problem of social reality,* M. Natanson (ed.). The Hague: Martinus Nijhoff.

Searle, J.
  1969   *Speech acts. An essay in the philosophy of language.* London: Cambridge University Press.
Seneca
  [63–65 ACE] 1962   *Epistulae morales.* R. M. Grummere, transl. Cambridge, Ma.: Harvard University Press.
Sjoberg, G.
  1961   *The preindustrial city.* Glencoe, Il.: The Free Press.
Spivak, G.
  1976   Introduction to J. Derrida, *Of grammatology.* Baltimore: The Johns Hopkins University Press.
Stoller, P.
  1977   Ritual and personal insults in Songrai sonni. *Anthropology* 2(1): 31–38.
  1978   *The dynamics of bankwano: Communication and legitimacy among the Songhay (Rep. of Niger).* Ph.D. Dissertation, Dept. of Anthropology, University of Texas at Austin.
  1980a   The epistemology of sorkotarey: Language, metaphor and healing among the Songhay. *Ethos* 8: 119–31.
  1980b   The negotiation of Songhay space: Phenomenology in the heart of darkness. *American Ethnologist* 7: 419–31.
  1981   Social interaction and the management of meaning among the Songhay. *Africa* 51: 765–80.
  1984a   Horrific comedy: Cultural resistance and the Hauka movement in Niger. *Ethos* 12: 165–87.
  1984b   Sound in Songhay cultural experience. *American Ethnologist* 11: 559–70.
  1984c   Eye, mind and word in anthropology. *L'Homme* 24: 91–114.
  1986   The reconstruction of ethnography. In P. Chock and J. Wyman (eds.) *Discourse and the social life of meaning.* Washington, D.C.: Smithsonian Institution Press: 51–74.
  1989   *Fusion of the worlds: An ethnography of possession among the Songhay of Niger.* Chicago: University of Chicago Press.
Stoller, P., and C. Olkes
  1986   Bad sauce, good ethnography. *Cultural Anthropology* 1: 336–52.
  1987   *In sorcery's shadow: A memoir of apprenticeship among the Songhay of Niger.* Chicago: University of Chicago Press.
Sturtevant, W.
  1968   Categories, percussion and physiology. *Man* (NS) 3: 133–34.
Sudnow, D. (ed.)
  1972   *Studies in social interaction.* New York: The Free Press.
Surugue, B.
  1972   *Contribution à l'étude de la musique sacrée Zarma-Songhay.* Etudes Nigeriennes #30. Niamey: Universite de Niamey.
Tambiah, S.
  1968   The magical power of words. *Man* (NS) 3: 175–203.
Tedlock, D.
  1982   Anthropological hermeneutics and the problem of alphabetic literacy. In J. Ruby (ed.) *A crack in the mirror: Reflective perspectives in anthropology.* Philadelphia: University of Pennsylvania Press: 149–61.

Tempels, P.
1949 *La philosophie Bantoue*. Paris: Présence Africaine.
Theroux, P.
1978 *The old Patagonian express*. Boston: Houghton-Mifflin.
Thompson, R. F.
1974 *African art in motion: Icon and art in the collection of Katherine Coryton White*. Berkeley: University of California Press.
Tisdale, C.
1979 *Joseph Beuys*. New York: Thames and Hudson.
Tyler, S.
1984 The vision quest in the West, or what the mind's eye sees. *Journal of Anthropological Research* 10: 23–41.
1986 Post-modern anthropology. In P. Chock and J. Wyman (eds.) *Discourse and the social life of meaning:* Washington, D.C.: Smithsonian Institution Press. 23–51.
1988 *The unspeakable*. Madison: University of Wisconsin Press.
Ulmer, G.
1985 *Applied grammatology*. Baltimore: The Johns Hopkins University Press.
Van Maanen, J.
1988 *Tales of the field: On writing ethnography*. Chicago: University of Chicago Press.
Wagner, R.
1981 *The invention of culture*. Chicago: University of Chicago Press.
Wallerstein, I.
1984 *The politics of the world economy*. New York: Cambridge University Press.
Williams, R.
1976 *Keywords: A vocabulary of culture and society*. New York: Oxford University Press.
White, D., M. Burton, and M. Dow
1981 Sexual division of labor in African agriculture: A network autocorrelation analysis. *American Anthropologist* 83: 824–50.
White, G. and C. Prachuabhmoh
1982 The cognitive organization of ethnic images. *Ethos* 11: 2–33.
Whitehead, A. N.
1969 *Process and reality*. New York: The Free Press.
Wober, M.
1966 Sensotypes. *The Journal of Social Psychology* 70: 181–89.
Zuckerkandl, V.
1956 *Sound and symbol: Music and the external world*. W. Trask, transl. Princeton, N.J.: Princeton University Press.

Films Cited

Rouch, J.
  1948   *Initiation à la danse des possédés*. Paris: Comité des Films Eth-
         nographiques.
Rouch, J.
  1949a *La circoncision*. Paris: Comité des Films Ethnographiques.
Rouch, J.
  1949b *Les Magiciens de Wanzerbé*. Paris: Comité des Films Ethnogra-
         phiques.
Rouch, J.
  1951   *Les Hommes qui font la pluie*. Paris: Comité des Films Ethno-
         graphiques.
Rouch, J.
  1954a *Les Maîtres fous*. Paris: Films de la Pléiade.
Rouch, J.
  1954b *Jaguar*. Paris: Films de la Pléiade.
Rouch, J.
  1957   *Moi, un noir*. Paris: Comité des Films Ethnographiques.
Rouch, J.
  1965   *Chasse au lion à l'arc*. Paris: Films de la Pléiade.
Rouch, J.
  1967   *Daouda Sorko*. Paris: Comité des Films Ethnographiques.
Rouch, J.
  1969   *Petit à petit*. Paris: Comité des Films Ethnographiques.
Rouch, J.
  1971   *Tourou et bitti*. Paris: Comité des Films Ethnographiques.
Rouch, J.
  1974   *Cocorico, monsieur poulet*. Paris: Comité des Films Ethnographi-
         ques.

Index